AMERICAN HERITAGE

June, 1968 · Volume XIX, Number 4

Benson J. Lossing was inspired to produce his best-selling Pictorial Field-Book of the Revolution *(1851–52) by hearing an aged veteran describe "Old Put's leap," which is depicted above in a spirited if somewhat primitive nineteenth-century painting. General Israel Putnam was interrupted by a British attack while shaving in a house near Greenwich, Connecticut, one morning in 1779. With lather still on his cheeks he mounted his horse and led an abortive defense before deciding upon an abrupt retreat by way of a flight of steps built into a steep hillside nearby. If we are to believe the unknown artist, Old Put's steed really stretched out and made it more or less in one jump. According to the original owner and commissioner of the painting, who used to exhibit it with other patriotic scenes, "the Brittish dragoons durst not follow the in tripid horseman down the precipice." An article about Lossing starts on page 54.*

AMERICAN HERITAGE

The Magazine of History

SENIOR EDITOR
Bruce Catton

EDITOR
Oliver Jensen

MANAGING EDITOR
Robert Lincoln Reynolds

ART DIRECTOR
Murray Belsky

ART EDITOR
Joan Paterson Kerr

ARTICLES EDITOR
E. M. Halliday

ASSOCIATE EDITORS
Robert S. Gallagher   David G. Lowe
Barbara Klaw   John L. Phillips
Douglas Tunstell

COPY EDITOR
Brenda Niemand

EDITORIAL ASSISTANTS
Mary Dawn Earley   Rosemary L. Klein
Mary A. Hawkins   Joanne Shapiro

PUBLISHER
Darby Perry

ADVISORY BOARD
Allan Nevins, *Chairman*
Carl Carmer   Louis C. Jones
Gerald Carson   Alvin M. Josephy, Jr.
Marshall B. Davidson   Howard H. Peckham
John A. Garraty   Francis S. Ronalds
Eric F. Goldman   S. K. Stevens

AMERICAN HERITAGE is published every two
months by American Heritage Publishing Co.,
Inc., 551 Fifth Avenue, New York, N.Y. 10017.

PRESIDENT
James Parton

CHAIRMAN, EDITORIAL COMMITTEE
Joseph J. Thorndike

MANAGING DIRECTOR, BOOK DIVISION
Richard M. Ketchum

SENIOR ART DIRECTOR
Irwin Glusker

Correspondence about subscriptions should be
sent to: American Heritage Subscription Office, 383 West Center Street, Marion, Ohio
43302. Single copies: $4.25. Annual subscrip-
tions: $16.50 in U.S. and Canada; $17.50 elsewhere. An annual Index of AMERICAN HERI-
TAGE is published in February, priced at $1.00.
AMERICAN HERITAGE will consider but assumes
no responsibility for unsolicited materials.
Title registered U.S. Patent Office. Second-
class postage paid at New York, N.Y., and
at additional mailing offices.

Sponsored by

American Association for State & Local History · Society of American Historians

CONTENTS *June, 1968 · Volume XIX, Number 4*

COVER: With little doubt the painter of this picture felt that he belonged to a great society whose future was assured. His name was Terence J. Kennedy, and his symbolic tribute to his country was made, presumably about 1840, in Auburn, New York. Under the wings of a native bird clearly akin to but built on a titanically larger scale than our AMERICAN HERITAGE eagle, the nation obviously thrives: ships steam and sail, canals flow, falls fall, flora flourish, and fauna feed, while symbols of industry—an anvil, a plow, a bobbin—pregnantly occupy the foreground. Somewhat tentatively (for it was too early to predict the railroad's dominance over American transportation) a locomotive pokes its nose into the picture from a tunnel just under the eagle's beak. The original painting now belongs to the New York State Historical Association, and is reproduced here by courtesy of *House Beautiful. Back Cover:* It is the nature of presidential campaign buttons to look confident; only in retrospect do the losers' emblems take on the sad luster of defeat. These four, from the collection of Stanley King, represent the leading contenders in 1948; their various fortunes in that surprising year are described in an article starting on page 22.

*This advertising broadside of the 1850's shows engravings
that identified as well as decorated particular Colt pistols.*

Samuel Colt's life was brief but eventful.
He was an imaginative inventor and
an ambitious pitchman whose legacy included scandal
and success—and firearms that were
revolutionary in more ways than one

Gunmaker to the World

By ELLSWORTH S. GRANT

The funeral of Samuel Colt, America's first great munitions maker, was spectacular—certainly the most spectacular ever seen in Hartford, Connecticut. It was like the last act of a grand opera, with threnodial music played by Colt's own band of immigrant German craftsmen, supported by a silent chorus of bereaved townsfolk. Crepe bands on their left arms, Colt's 1,500 workmen filed in pairs past the metallic casket in the parlor of Armsmear, his ducal mansion; then followed his guard—Company A, 12th Regiment, Connecticut Volunteers—and the Putnam Phalanx in their brilliant Continental uniforms.

A half mile away the largest private armory in the world stood quiet—its hundreds of machines idle, the revolvers and rifles on its test range silent. Atop the long dike protecting Colt's South Meadows development drooped the gray willows that furnished the raw material for his furniture factory. Beneath the dike a few skaters skimmed over the frozen Connecticut River. To the south, the complex of company houses was empty for the moment, as was the village specially built for his Potsdam willow workers.

On Armsmear's spacious grounds snow covered the deer park, the artificial lake, the statuary, the orchard, the cornfields and meadows, the fabulous greenhouses. At the stable, Mike Tracy, the Irish coachman, stood by Shamrock, the master's aged, favorite horse, and scanned the long line of sleighs and the thousands of bareheaded onlookers jamming Wethersfield Avenue. After the simple Episcopal service the workers formed two lines, through which the Phalanx solemnly marched—drums muffled, colors draped, and arms reversed. Behind them, eight pallbearers bore the coffin to the private graveyard near the lake.

Thus, on January 14, 1862, Colonel Samuel Colt was laid to rest, at the age of only forty-seven. At the time, he was America's best-known and wealthiest inventor, a man who had dreamed an ambitious dream and had made it come true. Sam Colt had raced through a life rich in controversy and calamity and had left behind a public monument and a private mystery. The monument, locally, was the Colt armory; in the world beyond, it was the Colt gun that was to pacify the western and southern frontiers and contribute much to their folklores. The mystery concerned his family, whose entanglements included lawsuits, murder, suicide, and possibly bigamy and bastardy. His had indeed been a full life.

On that January afternoon a kaleidoscope of colorful memories must have crowded the minds of the family and intimates who were present. The foremost mourner was the deceased's calm and composed young widow, Elizabeth, holding by the hand their three-year-old son Caldwell, the only one of five children to survive infancy. Elizabeth was to become Hartford's *grande dame,* and her elaborate memorials would ennoble Colt's deeds at the same time that they would help conceal the shadows of his past. Her mother, her sister Hetty, and her brothers Richard and John Jarvis, both Colt officials, sat behind her. Richard, then the dependable head of Colt's willow-furniture factory, would in a few years become the armory's third president. Only the year before, the Colonel had sent John to England to buy surplus guns and equipment. Colt had been extremely fond of both these men, in contrast to his tempestuous relationships with his own three brothers. Near the Jarvises sat Lydia Sigourney, Hartford's aging, prolific "sweet poetess," who had

Right: Samuel Colt looked every inch the industrial tycoon to Charles Loring Elliott, who also painted the widowed Elizabeth Hart Colt and son Caldwell (left) in 1865. The 1863 photograph above is of Samuel Caldwell Colt, the Colonel's nephew— or, perhaps, his illegitimate son.

been Colt's friend from his youth and who looked upon Mrs. Colt as "one of the noblest characters, having borne, like true gold, the test of both prosperity and adversity."

Four of the pallbearers had played major roles in Colt's fortunes. They were Thomas H. Seymour, a former governor of Connecticut; Henry C. Deming, mayor of Hartford; Elisha K. Root, mechanical genius and head superintendent of the armory; and Horace Lord, whom Colt had lured away from the gun factory of Eli Whitney, Jr., to become Root's right-hand man.

And in the background, obscured by the Jarvises and the Colt cousins, was a handsome young man named Samuel Caldwell Colt. In the eyes of the world he was the Colonel's favorite nephew and the son of the convicted murderer John Colt, but according to local gossip he was really the bastard son of the Colonel himself by a German mistress.

Hartford was stunned by Colt's early death. True, he had suffered for some time from gout and rheumatic fever; he had indulged fully in the pleasures of life; he had labored from dawn to dusk to the point of exhaustion; then, at Christmas, he had caught a cold and become delirious. Perhaps pneumonia had set in. Whatever the cause of the Colonel's death, the general reaction was, as one lady put it, that "the main spring is broken, and the works must run down."

Sam Colt had made his mark in Hartford—and in the world—in less than fourteen years, beginning with his return to his native city to achieve his life's ambition of having his own gun factory. In the two decades before that he had been a failure at school and in business, but not as an inventor, pitchman, and promoter of himself and his wares.

To many, his brash nature and new-fangled ideas made him seem an outsider—a wild frontiersman

rather than a sensible Yankee. Yet Sam's maternal grandfather, John Caldwell, had founded the first bank in Hartford, and his own father was a merchant speculator who had made and lost a fortune in the West Indies trade. Widowed when Sam was only seven—the year the boy took apart his first pistol—Christopher Colt had had to place his children in foster homes. At ten, Sam went to work in his father's silk mill at Ware, Massachusetts, and later spent less than two years at a private school at Amherst. Sam became in-

terested in chemistry and electricity, and fashioned a crude underwater mine filled with gunpowder and detonated from shore by an electric current carried through a wire covered with tarred rope. On July 4, 1829, he distributed a handbill proclaiming that "Sam'l Colt will blow a raft sky-high on Ware Pond." The youngster's experiment worked too well: the explosion was so great that water doused the villagers' holiday best. Angrily they ran after the boy, who was shielded by a young machinist whose name was Elisha Root.

8

This peaceful view of the Connecticut River and Colonel Samuel Colt's gun factory, with its distinctive blue cupola, was done about 1857 by an unknown American artist. The oval is one of a pair; the companion piece, painted from the southeast, is a view of Hartford with the Colt armory shown at the left. That painting served as our frontispiece twelve years ago this month.

Yearning for high adventure, Colt in 1830 persuaded his father to let him go to sea. It was arranged for him to work his passage on the brig *Corvo,* bound for London and Calcutta. "The last time I saw Sam," a friend wrote to Sam's father, "he was in tarpaulin [hat], checked shirt, checked trousers, on the fore topsail yard, loosing the topsail. . . . He is a manly fellow."

During this, his sixteenth year, Sam conceived, by observing the action of the ship's wheel, or possibly the windlass, a practical way for making a multishot pistol.

Probably from a discarded tackle block, he whittled the first model of a rotating cylinder designed to hold six balls and their charges. The idea was to enable the pawl attached to the hammer of a percussion gun to move as the gun was cocked, thus turning the cylinder mechanically. Colt thus became the inventor of what would be the definitive part of the first successful revolver. Although he later claimed he had not been aware of the existence of ancient examples of repeating firearms until his second visit to London in 1835,

9

it is likely that he had inspected them in the Tower of London in 1831, when the *Corvo* docked in the Thames. Moreover, he may have seen the repeating flintlock with a rotating chambered breech invented by Elisha Collier of Boston in 1813 and patented in England in 1818. But since Collier's gun was cumbersome and the cylinder had to be rotated by hand, Colt cannot be said to have copied its design.

Colt returned to Boston in 1831 with a model of his projected revolver. With money from his father he had two prototypes fabricated, but the first failed to fire and the second exploded. Out of funds, Sam had to scrimp to make his living and to continue the development of his revolver, which he was certain would make him a fortune. At Ware, his exposure to chemistry had introduced him to nitrous oxide, or laughing gas. Sam now set himself up as the "celebrated Dr. Coult of New York, London and Calcutta" and for three years toured Canada and the United States as "a practical chemist," giving demonstrations for which he charged twenty-five cents admission. Those who inhaled the gas became intoxicated for a few minutes; they would perform ludicrous feats, to the delight of the audience.

In the meantime, Colt had hired John Pearson of Baltimore to make improved models of his revolver, but he was at his wit's end trying to keep himself and the constantly grumbling Pearson going. Borrowing a thousand dollars from his father, Colt went to Europe and obtained patents in England and France. In 1836, aided by the U.S. commissioner of patents (a Hartford native named Henry Ellsworth), Colt received U.S. Patent No. 138, on the strength of which he persuaded a conservative cousin, Dudley Selden, and several other New Yorkers to invest some $200,000 to incorporate the Patent Arms Manufacturing Company of Paterson, New Jersey. Sam got an option to buy a third of the shares (though he was never able to pay for one of them), a yearly salary of $1,000, and a sizable expense account, of which he took full advantage to promote a five-shot revolver in Washington military and congressional circles. (The five-shooter was more practical to produce than a six-shot model based on Colt's original design.) At the time, the Army Ordnance Department, facing boldly backward, was satisfied with its single-shot breech-loading musket and flintlock pistol. A West Point competition rejected Colt's percussion-type arm as too complicated. Mean-

Part of the Colt munitions complex was destroyed by fire in February of 1864; the Aetna Insurance Company promptly incorporated the disaster into its advertising (left). Above is Armsmear, Colt's mansion; employee-inventor Charles Billings poses (right) in an armory band uniform.

while, Cousin Dudley was growing impatient with Sam's lavish dinner parties, lack of sales, and mounting debts. At one point he chastised Colt for his liquor bill: "I have no belief in undertaking to raise the character of your gun by old Madeira."

The clouds began to break in December of 1837, when Colonel William S. Harney, struggling to subdue the Seminole Indians in the Florida Everglades, ordered one hundred guns, stating, "I am . . . *confident* that they are the only things that will finish the *infernal war.*" Still, Colt failed to win over the stubborn head of Ordnance, Colonel George Bomford, until the summer of 1840, when another trial proved his gun's superiority and forced Bomford to give in slightly; Colt got an order for one hundred carbines at forty dollars apiece. It was a Pyrrhic victory, though, because sales were otherwise too meager to sustain the little company, and in September of 1842 its doors closed for good.

Colt wound up in debt and in controversy with his employers, whom he suspected of fiscal skulduggery. Disgusted with bureaucrats, he determined to be his own boss thereafter. To a member of the family he confided in his half-educated but colorful way:

To be a clerk or an office holder under the pay and patronage of Government, is to stagnate ambition & I hope by hevins I would rather be captain of a canal bote than have the biggest office in the gift of the Government . . . however inferior in wealth I may be to the many who surround me I would not exchange for there treasures the satisfaction I have in knowing I have done what has never before been accomplished by man. . . . Life is a thing to be enjoyed . . . it is the only certainty.

During this period Sam Colt was also involved in a trying and frustrating family tragedy. His erratic but usually mild older brother, John, who was struggling to earn a living by writing a textbook on bookkeeping, had rented a small office in New York City. Then, in September of 1841, he killed his irascible printer, Samuel Adams, after the two had fought over the accuracy of the printer's bill—their versions differed by less than twenty dollars. John (in self-defense, he claimed) struck Adams with a hatchet, then stuffed the body into a packing case and had it delivered to a

TEXT CONTINUED ON PAGE 86
A PORTFOLIO OF ILLUSTRATIONS BEGINS OVERLEAF

Catlin & Colt

Sam Colt was an aggressive merchandiser, and during the 1850's he arranged for George Catlin, the prominent and peripatetic painter of American Indians, to do a series of canvases to illustrate the use of Colt firearms in a variety of exotic settings. Six of the paintings were lithographed and widely distributed—and a powerful advertising campaign was launched. Four of the scenes in the following portfolio were actually part of the sextet; the others (the ostrich, flamingo, and jaguar hunts) were done in much the same general spirit and format—Catlin the hunter using Colt weaponry—but were not used to push the armory's line. The last illustration (pages 16 and 17) is a reproduction of one of the actual advertising lithographs, which today are quite rare. Apart from the zest of the paintings proper, Catlin's enthusiasm for his task is repeatedly borne out in passages from his *Life Among the Indians* and *Last Rambles Amongst the Indians of the Rocky Mountains and of the Andes,* both published in the 1860's. Catlin's was a breezy, freewheeling prose style; one of his favorite devices was to attribute personality to "Sam." "Sam! who's Sam?" he would challenge the reader in his chatty, rhetorical way. "Why *Sam Colt,* a six-shot little rifle, always lying *before* me during the day and *in my arms* during the night, by which a tiger's or alligator's eye, at a hundred yards, was sure to drop a red tear. . . ." During his South American travels Catlin disdained to use blowguns and poisoned arrows: "I don't wish to poison anybody! and game enough 'Sam' and I can always kill without it—powder and ball from Sam are *rank poison.*" So confident was Catlin of his armament ("made expressly for me by my old friend Colonel Colt," he proudly wrote) that, before an ostrich hunt in Argentina, he said he was reckoned a literal one-man band: "I . . . with 'Sam' in hand and a six-shot revolver in my belt, was considered equal to a war party." Faced with such vigorous testimonials—to say nothing of the exciting lithographs in the ads—what man of action could resist buying a Colt?

Catlin's Colt revolver fells a buffalo in Texas.

Catlin and "Sam" hunt ostriches in Argentina.

Catlin remains alert during a pause on Brazil's Rio Trombetas.

The artist tries to rescue a companion treed by peccaries.

Catlin portrayed himself as a mighty hunter of Texas flamingos.

Catlin nears his kill—a Brazilian jaguar.

The artist-hunter awes a group of Carib Indians with his repeating rifle.

By LOUIS M. STARR

Joseph Pulitzer and his most "indegoddampendent" editor

Frank Cobb often remained at his desk far into the night. He had to: Pulitzer expected editorials in the morning World *on all big stories, no matter how late they broke.*

Once there was an institution called, simply, the *World*. By the first decade of this century it had won a place in American life somewhat like that occupied by the *New York Times* today. It was the most influential newspaper in the biggest city in the land. Unlike the *Times,* which does not appeal to the masses, the *World* wore a double crown: it also had the most readers of any morning newspaper in the United States.

A chronic invalid who could not see well enough to sign his name owned the paper and ran it. Joseph Pulitzer set foot but twice in his gold-domed structure, briefly the tallest in Manhattan, an enormous sentinel guarding the business end of the Brooklyn Bridge. Yet the stamp of Pulitzer's volatile personality was on that building, on each of the some 1,800 men and women working there, on every edition of the morning, evening, and Sunday *Worlds* that poured out of it—especially the morning: *that* was the *World*.

Frank Irving Cobb was well aware of all this on Monday, May 9, 1904, the day he first rode one of the two big hydraulic elevators fourteen stories skyward to the editorial floor. Office lore had it that one of the first visitors to scale these heights, when the building opened in 1890, had peered into a door and inquired, "Is God in?" Cobb undoubtedly was more circumspect. Besides, he knew perfectly well that Pulitzer was away —at that moment soothing his embattled nerves at Aix-les-Bains in the French Alps. Cobb was greeted instead by William H. Merrill, the scholarly old editor, and introduced around as the newest member of the editorial staff. For a boy born in Shawnee County, Kansas, raised in the timber country of upper Michigan, and schooled on the newspapers of Grand Rapids and the still-hick town of Detroit, the altitude must have seemed a trifle giddy.

Frank Cobb would rue that day, and so would Joseph Pulitzer. Then again, both of them would later come almost to cherish it. It began a relationship that was stormy but productive, and at times even touching. It brought together the man commonly accounted the architect of the modern American newspaper, and his foremost editorialist.

Cobb, of course, was unknown, but in due course he would be considered by Woodrow Wilson and many other discerning readers as *the* editorial writer of his generation. An odd reflection of this is that when he died, members of the staff expressed genuine sympathy for the poor chap who had to succeed him, even though the successor was a bright prospect who had already made a mark: his name was Walter Lippmann. As for Pulitzer, by 1904 he rather enjoyed his status as

The fierce determination with which Joseph Pulitzer alternately inspired and terrorized his employees to editorial greatness is apparent in this portrait of the blind "Chief," painted in June, 1905, by John Singer Sargent.

a kind of half-remembered legend. Since he never appeared in public, a lot of people thought of him (as he himself noted, with sardonic humor) as long since dead. But there was no one who hadn't heard of him, or felt the impact of his work.

By birth Pulitzer was Hungarian, the well-tutored son of a Jewish grain merchant in Makó, who died

---

A great change has come over the American Negro's attitude toward the white man's government during the last four years. . . . He is no longer submissive but aggressive, and while this change has its grave dangers to the Negro himself, it is an inevitable consequence of the failure of local and State Governments to administer even-handed justice.

It is the fashion to attribute most of the recent race riots to economic rivalry between whites and blacks, but economic rivalry is no new thing . . . and this conflict is bound to go on as long as the two races compete for their daily bread. Rivalry, however, is not riot, and back of all these miniature civil wars which disgrace the Nation from year to year is the breakdown of government and the denial of due process of law to the Negro.

Lincoln said that this government could not endure half slave and half free. It cannot endure with one law for the white man and another law for the black man. There must be one law for both, and until there is one law for both every community of mixed population is living under the shadow of threatened anarchy.

Cobb in the *World,* June 3, 1921

---

young, and of a Catholic mother, who soon remarried. At seventeen, he arrived in this country in time to serve in Mr. Lincoln's army during the final months of the Civil War. Then he roustabouted in St. Louis. He worked ferociously for a German-language paper there, studying English on the side. By the time he reached New York, still in his mid-thirties, this wiry, nervous apparition had served in the Missouri legislature; courted and married Kate Davis, a distant, aristocratic, and quite ravishing cousin of the former Confederate president; and bought himself a decrepit evening paper at auction and immediately merged it with a fearful competitor's to form the St. Louis *Post-Dispatch,* which he turned into a lusty, crusading sheet that minted money. In the course of all this, Pulitzer had absorbed the ideas and ideals of democracy to an extent that, to the more sober burghers of the time and place, seemed positively alarming.

Upon this apparent chump Jay Gould, the fancy financier, performed the characteristic feat of unload-

ing a losing property for which he no longer had use, the New York *World.* To the surprise of almost everyone, notably Gould, Charles Anderson Dana of the *Sun,* James Gordon Bennett, Jr., of the *Herald,* Whitelaw Reid of the *Tribune,* and the solemn proprietors of the *Times,* the *World* became the biggest thing of its kind within two years. Pulitzer accomplished this with a bewildering mixture of political and general news, crime reports, crusades, stunts, human-interest stories in which women in various forms of distress and disarray predominated, plenty of illustrations of these and other matters of interest, cartoons, and editorials that thundered at the plutocrats and exalted democracy. The *World's* climb gained extra spurts through such Pulitzer strokes as promoting Grover Cleveland for President before others gave him a tumble and (more memorably) converting the erection and dedication of the Statue of Liberty into a triumphant *World* promotion by raising from its readers the money for the pedestal which Congress had failed to appropriate. (Thenceforth a vignette of the statue graced the *World's* nameplate, lest anyone forget.)

Swift success was followed by personal tragedy. Exhausted by a political campaign in November, 1887, Pulitzer was struck down by nervous prostration and a detached retina in his one sound eye. The rest of his life became a nightmare of doctors' consultations, insomnia, monumental headaches, asthma, chronic indigestion, nerves that jolted him at the first hint of noise, fits of rage and of despondency. Pulitzer, a man of explosive energy, endured all this while trapped in a twilight that faded slowly into total darkness.

From the first, the doctors agreed on one point: he must stay away from the *World,* the farther the better. Pulitzer obeyed, but after a few disastrous attempts at cutting himself off altogether, he contrived to keep in touch with his paper no matter where he was—usually at Bar Harbor in summer, in Europe during spring and fall, at Jekyll Island, Georgia, in winter, and (dangerously) in New York between seasons. Others edited, sold the advertising, signed the contracts for newsprint and presses. But the voluminous Pulitzer papers now at Columbia University testify that matters of moment down to the hiring of an assistant city editor, and many that were of no moment, were settled by a telegram, cable, or memorandum signed "J. P."

Thus Pulitzer and Cobb were apart most of the time, and that was a mercy. They possessed, said a witness of their relationship, "much the same vociferousness of manner, headlong speech, and trick of over-assertion." He might have added other explosive characteristics they shared: savage independence in politics, contempt for mediocrity, fluency in the art of cursing (H. L. Mencken's *American Language* credits

J. P. with "indegoddampendent"), and a fierce devotion to the proposition—one hopes it does not sound quaint—that a daily newspaper damned well ought to be a mighty engine of social progress.

Pulitzer already knew about the new boy in school. J. P. had been hunting a successor to Merrill, whom he had taken to addressing as "My Dear Old Man" for more than two years. In typical Pulitzer fashion, the search became exasperatingly thorough. He had commanded Don Seitz, his able lieutenant, to send him reports on every editorial writer in New York. None would do. Seitz and others had scanned out-of-town papers fruitlessly. When Samuel M. Williams, one of J. P.'s favorite reporters, bet that he could find the right man, Pulitzer dispatched him forthwith on a cross-country quest that ended with a few spirited lines he found in the Detroit *Free Press*. Williams tracked down the author and sent an enthusiastic report to J. P., only to be ordered to interview the innocent prospect again and yet again. What did this Cobb look like? What had he read? What did he know about American history? How were his table manners? "Search his brain," Pulitzer told Williams, "for everything there is in it." And please send more editorials.

The word from Detroit was that Frank Cobb looked like a lumberjack, which was logical, because that was what he had been. Big, powerfully built, and carelessly dressed, he had a thatch of tousled hair that obscured a broad brow; his eyes were straightforward and intelligent, his jaw becomingly belligerent. As to his reading, writing, and table manners, the President of the United States could testify. Passing through Detroit once, Theodore Roosevelt had been so taken by a Cobb editorial on the unlikely subject of Scandinavian literature that he too had inquired for the author and had him to lunch. On another occasion, Cobb had challenged T. R. on some point of American history now lost to the ages, and carried the day.

Pulitzer absorbed all this, and listened impatiently to batches of Cobb editorials read to him in relays by the harried young men who served him as secretaries. Back went the verdict. Cobb was "too prolix . . . not incisive, terse, and direct enough." Let Williams tell him so—test number one. Cobb retorted, "Few newspaper publishers are willing to give an editorial writer *time* to be brief. . . . I sometimes think the time varies inversely with the square of the length." J. P. summoned him to Jekyll Island that March, then sent word to Merrill that, come May, Cobb was to go on trial at $100 a week.

The probation lasted about two years and included, along with several raises and some compliments, comments by Pulitzer that he had to leave the room for a breath of air after listening to Cobb's efforts; that they

made him sick (a colloquialism he used frequently and often meant literally); that Seitz should present to Cobb a beautifully made set of miniature silver scales as a reminder to weigh his words more meticulously; that Cobb's irony turned out as flippancy; that he was guilty of "silly schoolboy recklessness, overzeal and lack of restraint"; and that (on the other hand) he tended to favor a remote academic issue over a "concrete, burning one." For his part, Cobb on at least one occasion chose to ignore J. P.'s orders for an editorial. When Pulitzer inquired pointedly at what hour his instructions had been delivered, Cobb wrote Seitz that he could inform the boss they had arrived at 11 P.M., and, "not being a damned fool," he had not attempted an editorial at that hour; Cobb expressed resentment at "insinuations that he is neglecting his work," and said he had "no excuses or apologies to offer."

By December of his first year, the new boy knew he would be around for a while. Old Merrill dutifully reported to Pulitzer that he had read at least thirty

---

The World Almanac *for 1920 has already been printed and tens of thousands of copies have been distributed and cannot be recalled; but the Almanac again contains the Declaration of Independence, and the new Sedition Bill as agreed to by the House Judiciary Committee provides that any person shall be deemed guilty of a felony* "who either orally or by writing, printing or . . . shall otherwise teach, incite, advocate, propose or advise, or aid, abet or encourage forcible resistance to or destruction of the Government of the United States. . . ."

Now, unfortunately, the second paragraph of the Declaration of Independence is defiantly seditious. . . . The World can easily suppress the Declaration of Independence in all future editions of the Almanac, but in the mean time the mischief has been done for 1920 and the seditious utterances of Thomas Jefferson have been scattered to the four corners of the country.

For any evil consequences that may ensue . . . we can only beg for mercy and for such consideration as the Department of Justice may graciously grant. . . .

January 13, 1920

---

editorials in other papers on Roosevelt's annual message to Congress, and "not one of them seemed to me equal to Cobb's in discrimination, fairness, and style. . . . I do not know of so capable and promising a *young man* for the first place." Seitz and others were equally enthusiastic. J. P. ordered that Cobb be signed to a three-year contract and had him come by for a talk.

The result was that Cobb was to take turns at run-

CONTINUED ON PAGE 82

The President's popularity was waning, and he
was facing an able Republican as well as two
rebels from his own party. At hand was the

1948 ELECTION

with the nation in peril at home and abroad.
Then Harry S. Truman set out to give 'em hell.

By ROBERT SHOGAN

Even by the standards of blasé Washington, it was an impressive affair. The date was February 19, 1948. The occasion was one of the great ritual feasts of the Democratic party, the annual Jefferson-Jackson Day dinner. The 2,100 guests filled two of the capital's grandest banquet halls—the Presidential Room of the Hotel Statler and the ballroom of the Mayflower Hotel. The distinguished company included President Harry S. Truman and the First Lady, members of the Cabinet, and sundry senators and representatives. They dined on terrapin soup and breast of capon and toasted their nineteenth-century patron saints in champagne.

But the minds of the Democratic leaders were fixed on the future. Specifically, they were looking ahead to the presidential election less than nine months away. They calculated that—at $100 a plate plus "additional contributions"—the dinner guests would donate more than $250,000 toward the millions needed to finance the fall campaign. And in anticipation of the July nominating convention, the after-dinner entertainment included a "draft-Truman" rally, complete with placards reading: "Harry Is Our Date in '48." Later, the sixty-three-year-old President delivered the main address, which the radio networks broadcast to the nation.

No effort was spared that evening to convey to the American public the image of an enthusiastic and united party. But no one knew better than the Democratic chieftains themselves how false this picture was. The painful truth was that not since Al Smith's disastrous defeat in 1928 had the party's prestige been so low and its prospects so bleak.

The Democratic malaise was occasioned by the colossal problems that confronted the country after the end of World War II. Victory found the economy dislocated, much of the population uprooted (more than twelve million men were still in uniform), and frustration with wartime rigors and controls near the breaking point. Organized labor, whose wage demands had been tightly reined for nearly four years, could be held back no longer. Their right to strike now restored, the big unions—the auto workers, the steel workers, the packing-house workers, the electrical workers, the mine workers—all walked out. By the end of 1946 the total production time lost to strikes had tripled the previous annual record.

The resulting wage hikes added to the pressure mounting within the business community for higher prices. Finally, in the spring of 1946, Congress stripped the wartime Office of Price Administration of nearly all its power; between June 15 and July 15 food prices soared nearly fifteen per cent, the largest monthly jump ever recorded by the Bureau of Labor Statistics. Still, industry could not catch up with the pent-up demand for autos, apartments, and a host of other scarce items. In desperation, consumers turned to the black market, which flourished as it never had in wartime.

Even as they contended with these domestic headaches, Americans cast worried glances abroad. The peace they had just won was suddenly in deadly peril. Soviet Russia, a wartime ally, now loomed as a dangerous adversary. In Fulton, Missouri, Winston S. Churchill described the geographical dimensions of the Iron Curtain, behind which Stalin massed his troops. Should he give the order to march, there seemed little to stop the Red Army from engulfing Europe and the Middle East.

In the twelve tumultuous months after V-J Day, the sense of victory had dissipated, and the ruling Democratic party suffered the consequences. The Republicans exploited the national mood in the 1946 congressional elections with a provocative slogan. "Had enough?" they asked. The electorate answered by unseating dozens of Democratic lawmakers and giving the Republican party control of both houses of Congress for the first time since 1928.

So demoralized was the party of Jefferson and Jackson that on the day after the 1946 balloting, J. William Fulbright, the junior senator from Arkansas, proposed that Harry Truman resign after appointing a Republican Secretary of State to succeed him. "It will place the responsibility of running the Government on one party and prevent a stalemate," Fulbright explained. Truman promptly labelled Fulbright "half-bright" and indignantly rejected his proposal. But the feeling grew, among both Democrats and Republicans, that if Truman did not quit the White House the voters would turn him out.

Certainly little had happened between the 1946 elections and early 1948 to brighten the postwar situation. With the Truman Doctrine, the United States had pledged to help Greece and Turkey resist Communist aggression. And through the Marshall Plan it had committed its economic might to aid in the rebuilding of all of Western Europe. But still the Old World teetered on the brink of chaos; and halfway around the globe, Chiang Kai-shek was waging a losing battle to keep China from falling under Communist domination. At home, the pressures of the postwar era were shattering the grand Democratic coalition that Franklin Roosevelt had forged and led to victory in four national elections.

The disintegration had begun on the left flank.

Convinced that the tough new stance the United States had assumed toward the Soviet Union would lead to war, Henry Agard Wallace announced in December, 1947, that he would run for President on a third-party ticket. Wallace had been Roosevelt's Secretary of Agriculture for almost eight years and his Vice President for four more. Many regarded him, rather than Truman, as F. D. R.'s true political heir. Indeed, at the Democratic convention in 1944, Wallace had come close to being renominated as Vice President. That Wallace was still a potent political figure the Democrats had learned from the results of a special congressional election in New York City only two days before the Jefferson-Jackson Day dinner. The candidate backed by Wallace had won a stunning upset victory over one of the country's most powerful Democratic machines.

Just as left-wing Democrats were disturbed by Truman's foreign policy, the party's southern conservatives were up in arms over his approach to a major domestic issue—civil rights. The great economic and social upheaval accompanying the war had given some fifteen million American Negroes new hope and aspirations. To help alleviate the Negro's long-neglected grievances, Truman that very month had sent to Congress a bold legislative program asking for federal laws against lynching, the poll tax, and discrimination in employment. The reaction in the South was immediate. Southern governors meeting in Florida at the time called for an "all-South" political convention and warned: "The President must cease attacks on white supremacy or face full-fledged revolt in the South." Judging from the number of southerners absent from the Jefferson-Jackson Day dinner, the revolt seemed to be under way already. Senator Olin Johnston of South Carolina even reserved an entire table in a prominent position in the banquet hall, then sent an aide to make sure the table remained pointedly vacant.

If the Democrats were to survive as a national political force, let alone stand a chance in the 1948 elections, they needed a leader strong enough to rally the party regulars and to put down the rebellions that threatened on left and right. It was a challenge that would have sorely tried even Franklin Roosevelt. And most knowledgeable politicians agreed that it was a task far beyond the capacities of Harry S. Truman.

No one had intended Truman to be President of the United States, least of all Truman himself. In fact, he had not much wanted to be Vice President. His ascent to the White House was marked by two fateful phone calls. The first came during the 1944 Democratic convention in Chicago, when the party faced a bitter fight over the vice-presidential nomination. On one side were the liberal supporters of incumbent Vice President Wallace; on the other were the conservative backers of James Byrnes of South Carolina, a former senator and Supreme Court justice and then the director of War Mobilization. Truman seemed a logical compromise. He had been a senator from Missouri for ten years and had distinguished himself during an investigation of mismanagement of the war effort. But Truman insisted that he was not a candidate. Finally, Democratic National Chairman Robert Hannegan summoned the reluctant senator to his hotel suite. While they talked, the phone rang. It was the President, demanding to know if Hannegan had "got that fellow lined up yet?"

"He is the contrariest Missouri mule I've ever dealt with," Hannegan complained.

"Well, you tell him," F. D. R. bellowed, loud enough for Truman to hear, "that if he wants to break up the Democratic party in the middle of a war, that's his responsibility."

After that, there was nothing for Truman to do but accept his fate. He dutifully pitched in during the fall campaign and after inauguration day quietly accepted

A NATIONAL DILEMMA

The Soviet blockade of Berlin in June, 1948, led President Truman to initiate the most massive airlift in history. But Dewey refused to make political capital of either the cold war abroad or the sensational charges of subversion at home made by Whittaker Chambers (right) to the House Un-American Activities Committee. Chambers' prime target, Alger Hiss, is laughing, upper left.

FENNO JACOBS—BLACK STAR

WIDE WORLD. PAGE 22: UPI; PAGE 23: WIDE WORLD

the obscurity to which the President relegated him.

Truman had been Vice President of the United States less than three months when, on April 12, 1945, he received the second momentous phone call. Presidential Press Secretary Steve Early told Truman that he was wanted immediately at the White House. Truman dashed over to find Eleanor Roosevelt waiting for him. "Harry," she said, "the President is dead." Ninety minutes later, Truman was sworn in as the thirty-third President of the United States.

"Boys, if you ever pray, pray for me now," the new President told the White House press corps. "I don't know whether you fellows ever had a load of hay fall on you, but when they told me yesterday what had happened, I felt like the moon, the stars, and all the planets had fallen on me."

At first, as the United States went about finishing off the Axis powers, the new Commander in Chief's modesty and matter-of-fact manner struck just the right note. But this harmonious state of affairs had already begun to deteriorate by the time victory was achieved. Not unnaturally, as postwar problems cropped up, the Chief Executive became the target of mounting criticism.

"To err is Truman," the wiseacres jeered. The President was roundly criticized not only for his handling of major issues of domestic and foreign policy but even for minor notions that seized his fancy. When he proposed to build a new balcony on the White House, the New York *Herald Tribune* upbraided him "for meddling with a historic structure which the nation prefers as it is." Underlying much of the fault-finding was a complaint that the President could do little about. Many Americans simply could not forgive Harry Truman for not being Franklin Roosevelt.

In thirteen years F. D. R. had left an indelible mark on the Presidency. Inevitably Truman was compared to his predecessor, a comparison that nearly always worked to his disadvantage. A bitter jest summed up the difference between the Hyde Park squire and the son of the Middle Border: "For years we had the champion of the common man in the White House. Now we have the common man."

Roosevelt, with his leonine head and patrician features, was a strikingly handsome man. Truman, with his square-cut midwestern face and thick-lensed glasses, was undistinguished in appearance. Roosevelt's manner was the epitome of elegance and grace; Truman's bearing brought to mind a shopkeeper—which, it was remembered, he had been, and a bankrupt one at that. In no comparison did Truman suffer more than when it came to oratory. Roosevelt's sonorous tones and superb timing had enhanced his eloquence;

Truman's rasping monotone seemed to dull the edge of every point his speech writers sought to make.

His performance at the 1948 Jefferson-Jackson Day dinner was all too typical of what Americans had come to expect from their President. Truman's address lasted only twenty-two minutes, but it seemed a good deal longer to many in the audience; at the head table Leslie Biffle, secretary for the Senate minority and one of Truman's closest friends, dozed off.

Halfway through his address, Mr. Truman tried to rouse his audience by poking fun at the "reactionaries" who opposed his program. "These men who live in the past remind me of a toy . . . called the 'floogie bird,'" the President said. "Around the floogie bird's neck is a label reading: 'I fly backwards. I don't care where I'm going. I just want to see where I've been.'" The laughter was scarcely uproarious, and understandably so. Only two months before, Henry Wallace had told the same story about the "oozle finch." And before that, Franklin Roosevelt had given Republicans the same bird, which he called the "dodo."

Listening to the President tell his warmed-over joke, mindful of the decline in his popularity, the assembled Democrats may very well have considered Truman an albatross hung on their necks which would drag them and their party down to overwhelming defeat in November.

These features of the political landscape that the Democrats perceived with such foreboding were, of course, equally apparent to the Republicans, who were unanimously convinced that 1948 was the year when a Republican would at last return to the White House. But which Republican? The Grand Old Party, like the Democrats, had to contend with a bitter intramural dispute between its eastern liberals and its midwestern Old Guard.

The dominant faction appeared to be the liberals. On major domestic issues their differences with the Democrats were more procedural than substantive; on foreign policy their disagreements were almost nonexistent. Their candidate was Thomas E. Dewey, who at forty-six had been governor of New York for six years and a national figure for a decade. Dewey had risen to prominence in the 1930's as a racket-busting district attorney in New York City. At the 1940 convention he had led the race for the nomination before being swept aside by the boom for Wendell L. Willkie. But this setback was only temporary. In 1942 Dewey became the first Republican in twenty years to win the governorship of New York. In Albany, a traditional forcing ground for presidential timber, Dewey established a reputation as a moderate on economic and social problems, and as an exceptionally efficient manager of the state's bureaucracy. In foreign affairs he moved from isolationism to active support of the United Nations. By 1944 Dewey's prestige was so great and his political staff so adroit that he won the Republican nomination without openly campaigning for it.

In the election he could not overcome Franklin Roosevelt's great personal popularity or the electorate's reluctance to depose a Commander in Chief during wartime. But Dewey made a better showing than any of Roosevelt's previous Republican opponents. And this respectable defeat was followed by an impressive victory in 1946 that returned him to the governor's mansion in Albany.

Dewey was not a dramatic or compelling figure. His critics found his manner cold and smug. Harold Ickes, the former Secretary of the Interior under Roosevelt and Truman, caustically likened Dewey to "the little man on the wedding cake" and said he reminded him of someone "who, when he had nothing to do, went home and cleaned his bureau drawers." But Dewey had a rich baritone voice, ideal for radio; he was clean cut and well groomed; and he combined youthful vigor with the political seasoning gained in the 1944 presidential campaign. All these things, the liberal Republicans felt, made Dewey the party's logical choice for 1948.

Stubbornly arrayed against the Dewey forces was the conservative Old Guard of the Republican party. Its ranks were made up of party stalwarts whose efforts held the Republican machinery together between national elections. Their roots were in the Midwest hinterland, their views harked back to William McKinley, and their champion in 1948 was Robert Alphonso Taft of Ohio. The son of the conservative Republican President, the fifty-eight-year-old Taft had emerged as a formidable political figure. He had proved his skill as a political tactician in the Senate, where he was *de facto* leader of his party. More than that, to conservatives Taft had come to symbolize thrift, honor, patriotism, and other old-fashioned virtues that they felt had been subordinated during two decades of bewildering change.

Taft was a shy, sour-looking man, almost totally lacking in personal magnetism. Too often his comments on controversial issues were blunt and politically ill-considered. In 1947, for instance, he advised Americans confronted with skyrocketing food prices to "eat less," a comment that predictably brought a chorus of derision from the Democrats. But despite his faults, or perhaps because of them, Taft remained the hero of the Old Guard and the most serious threat to Dewey's nomination.

The very fact that the GOP had two contenders as strong as Dewey and Taft, in a year when Republican chances seemed so bright, kindled the hopes of a number of lesser men who hoped that the party might turn to one of them in the event of a convention stalemate. Prominent among those being groomed as Republican dark horses in the winter of 1947–48 were General Douglas MacArthur, then the American proconsul in Japan; Senator Arthur Vandenberg of Michigan, one of the chief architects of the nation's bipartisan foreign policy; the very popular Governor Earl Warren of California; and Joe Martin of Massachusetts, Speaker of the House in the Republican Eightieth Congress.

But by far the most vigorous dark-horse candidate was Harold Stassen. In 1938, Stassen had startled the nation by winning the governorship of Minnesota when he was only thirty-one. Two years later he had been Willkie's floor leader at the Republican convention. After wartime service in the Navy, Stassen had returned to the political scene more ambitious than ever. In December, 1946, he became the first Republican to declare his candidacy for the Presidency and then launched a campaign that was eventually to cover 160,000 miles in forty-two states. As a midwesterner, Stassen had some appeal for conservatives, while liberals found his internationalist views attractive. But

A NATIONAL DISGRACE

The southern wing of the Democratic party deserted Truman because of his advocacy of the civil-rights cause, but the President more than made up this loss by the support he received from America's increasingly restive Negro minority, some of whom are shown listening to him at a rally in New York's Harlem.

CORNELL CAPA—*Life*

unlike Dewey and Taft, he had no backlog of delegate strength that he could count on at the convention. His only chance for the nomination was to make an impressive showing in the preconvention primaries, and accordingly he entered nearly all of these.

In March of 1948, Stassen lost the opening round to Dewey in New Hampshire. But the result was not significant, because Dewey was operating near his home base and with the backing of the New Hampshire Republican organization. In the next primary, in Wisconsin, where Dewey enjoyed no such advantages and made only a token effort, the returns told a different story. Stassen scored a smashing victory, winning nineteen delegates to eight for MacArthur and none for Dewey.

The Wisconsin vote had two immediate results in the battle for the nomination. Because of his poor showing in what was nominally his home state, MacArthur was eliminated from serious consideration. Dewey, who until then had not taken the primaries seriously, was forced to change his strategy. He suddenly broke away from Albany and plunged headlong into campaigning for the Nebraska primary, which followed Wisconsin's by seven days. But Stassen had been barnstorming in Nebraska at a furious pace for weeks, and it was too late for Dewey to catch up. Nebraska Republicans gave Stassen forty-three per cent of their vote to thirty-five per cent for Dewey.

On the strength of his primary victories, Stassen jumped ahead of Dewey in the Gallup poll. Next was the Oregon primary, where another Stassen triumph would make it almost impossible for the party to deny him the prize he sought. The Oregon polls showed Stassen had a commanding lead.

Dewey was finally alerted and ready for a fight. Three weeks before the balloting, the New Yorker swept into Oregon and began campaigning by bus in every corner of the state. No hamlet was too small for Dewey to visit, no hand too humble to shake. As Dewey poured it on, it was Stassen's turn to become alarmed. In his panic, he made a crucial error. He challenged Dewey to a debate on whether the Communist party should be outlawed; Stassen offered to take the affirmative.

Dewey eagerly accepted. His courtroom experience proved ideal training for such an encounter. While voters around the country listened in on their radios, the ex-district attorney tore Stassen's arguments to bits. After that, Oregon's verdict at the polls was no surprise. Dewey not only captured the state's twelve convention delegates but also greatly increased his prestige across the nation on the eve of the Republican convention.

More than 2,000 delegates and alternates convened in Philadelphia on June 21, and the day marked the dawn of a new political age. Television had arrived. The cameras transmitted the deliberations at Convention Hall to the largest audience in history ever to witness an event as it was happening. The eighteen stations that beamed the proceedings "live" reached ten million potential viewers from Boston to Richmond. And beyond the range of the East Coast cable system, millions more watched filmed highlights a day or two later.

All this foreshadowed the time when television would reshape the conduct of the conventions and completely transform the face of national politics. But in 1948 the medium was still a novelty with limited reach—there were in all the United States only about one million TV sets, and most of these were in bars. Besides, at the 1948 Republican convention, as at most political gatherings, the major decisions were being made well out of camera range.

Dewey arrived in Philadelphia with 350 votes, gathered in open primaries and behind-the-scenes maneuverings. The New York governor needed about 200 more to secure his nomination. Conceivably, he could be stopped if his foes united behind one man. But that would take time, and time was running out.

While Stassen, Taft, Vandenberg, and the others bickered among themselves, Dewey's emissaries went forth to the headquarters of uncommitted delegations, wheedling, cajoling, and promising—or at least seeming to promise. Rumors swept through the delegates' ranks that the Dewey forces had mortgaged the Vice Presidency to one influential figure or another in return for his support. One state after another wavered and then, fearful of being bypassed by the Dewey bandwagon, panicked and climbed aboard.

On the first ballot Dewey had 434 votes, just 114 short of the needed majority. Taft had 224 votes and Stassen 157, with the rest scattered among half a dozen favorite sons. Then came the crucial second round. To maintain the psychological pressure, Dewey's lead would have to grow; it did, to 515 votes, only 33 short of nomination.

While the convention recessed, Taft put through a desperate phone call to Stassen. The only chance to stop Dewey, Taft argued, was for Stassen to release his delegates to Taft. No, said Stassen, not until the fourth ballot. But Taft now knew there would be no fourth ballot. Connecticut and California were both ready to switch to Dewey, and that would be more than enough to put him over the top. Wearily, Taft scribbled a few lines and put through another phone call, this time to Ohio's other senator, John Bricker, who had placed Taft's name in nomination (and who had been Dewey's running mate in 1944). Just before the third ballot began, Bricker read Taft's message to the convention: "Dewey is a great Republican, and he will make a great Republican President."

A tremendous roar greeted the announcement, and within a few minutes the other candidates also bowed out. On the third ballot Dewey became his party's unanimous choice.

To the wild cheers of the delegates, Dewey entered the hall and began his brief acceptance speech with a statement that nearly rocked some of his listeners out of their seats. "I come to you," Dewey declared, "unfettered by a single obligation or promise to any living person."

The delegates who had been privy to the intensive preballoting bargaining conducted by Dewey's lieutenants found it hard to reconcile what they had witnessed with what they now heard. But it was soon clear that Dewey meant exactly what he said, at least when it came to the Vice Presidency. Whatever promises his aides might have made or implied would not be binding on him.

Dewey did confer for several hours with the leaders of his party on vice-presidential possibilities. Not until the meeting was over did the candidate register his view, which turned out to be the only one that counted. At 4 A.M., he summoned Earl Warren to his hotel and offered him the Vice Presidency. In 1944 Dewey had made the same offer, but Warren, who cherished his own presidential ambitions for 1948, had turned him down. Now the circumstances were far different. Warren could not again turn Dewey down and still retain standing in his party. After receiving Dewey's promise to invest the Vice Presidency with

meaningful responsibility, Warren agreed to run.

The Republicans thus offered the electorate the governors of the two richest and most populous states, men whose achievements commanded the respect of voters in both parties. The ticket spanned the nation from coast to coast, and along with geographic balance, presented a fortunate combination of personalities. Warren's good-natured warmth nicely complemented Dewey's brisk, chilly manner. All things considered, it seemed that the Republicans had come up with their strongest possible ticket.

Its potency only reinforced the general opinion among politicians that the Democratic cause was hopeless. Truman, who in March had publicly announced that he would seek to succeed himself, vigorously disagreed, but most observers concluded that the President was simply out of touch with reality.

Typical was the view expressed by Ernest K. Lindley, *Newsweek*'s Washington columnist, shortly before the Democratic convention. "The cold facts of the political situation are in many ways unjust to Harry Truman," Lindley wrote, "but they cannot be removed by wishful thinking or personal pluck. The most popular, and probably the best, service that Truman could render to his party now is to step aside and . . . to assist in vesting the party leadership in younger hands."

Truman had no intention of doing any such thing. He had, he liked to point out, waged uphill fights before. Back in 1940, as his first term in the Senate drew to a close, he had been faced with political extinction. The Pendergast machine in Kansas City, which had launched him into politics as a county judge (an administrative, not judicial, position) in 1922 and which

ALL: UPI

THREE
NATIONAL ISSUES

Labor did not forget Truman's veto, overridden by a Republican Congress, of the hated Taft-Hartley Bill. Meanwhile, the President picked up decisive votes across the country by successfully blaming that same "do-nothing" Congress for a housing shortage, which had forced many families into makeshift quarters, and for falling farm prices, which were partly the result of inadequate government storage facilities for the bumper grain crop.

had helped send him to the U. S. Senate in 1934, had been wrecked by federal tax investigators. Its leader, Tom Pendergast, had been jailed for income-tax evasion. Truman, loyal to Boss Tom until the end, found himself discredited and with no other political base. Truman was advised to withdraw from the contest for the Democratic senatorial nomination and to accept an appointment to the Interstate Commerce Commission tendered by Franklin Roosevelt. Truman indignantly refused the offer and hurled himself into a bitter primary campaign. With the last-minute help of the railroad unions, grateful for his work on railroad labor legislation, Truman squeaked through to victory in the primary and then handily defeated the Republicans in November.

His 1940 triumph gave Truman abundant confidence as a campaigner and political tactician. In 1948, as he considered his chances of remaining in the White House, his confidence was bolstered by his understanding of the Presidency. No President, not even F. D. R., had a keener appreciation of the powers of the office or a greater willingness to use them than Truman. He had brought the Second World War to an end by ordering the first atomic bomb dropped. In the midst of the postwar labor unrest he had staved off a national railroad strike by threatening to draft the trainmen into the army. And with the Truman Doctrine and the Marshall Plan he had involved the United States in an unprecedented overseas commitment to save the peace.

It mattered little to Truman if the press and Congress objected to what he did. The decisive judgment, as he saw it, rested with the people, who were the ultimate source of presidential power. "I have always believed that the vast majority of people want to do what is right," Truman said later, "and that if the President is right and can get through to the people he can always persuade them."

His campaign to carry "a personal message" to the people began when he accepted the offer of an honorary degree from the University of California, which enabled him to list the trip as "nonpolitical" and to have it paid for by the federal treasury rather than by the impecunious Democratic National Committee. On June 3 he set off by special train for the West Coast on a journey that took him across eighteen states, with stops for major addresses in five key cities and more than three score off-the-cuff rear-platform talks. Everywhere he went, Truman jauntily announced that he was on his way "fur to get me a degree." Having established the nonpolitical pretext for the trip, Truman then got down to his personal message: "There is just one big issue. It is the special interests against the peo-

ple, and the President being elected by all the people represents the people." Who represented the special interests? Why, the Republican party, of course, and most particularly the Republican-controlled Eightieth Congress. "You've got the worst Congress in the United States you've ever had," the President declared. "If you want to continue the policies of the Eightieth Congress, it'll be your funeral."

It was on this trip that the first shouts of "Give 'em hell, Harry!"—soon to become the battle cry of the Democratic campaign—were heard. Truman later claimed that it was originated by "some man with a great big voice" in Seattle. "I told him at that time and I have been repeating it ever since, that I have never deliberately given anybody hell. I just tell the truth on the opposition—and they think it's hell."

The spectacle of the President of the United States rampaging across the land, spewing hell-fire and brimstone at them, and all at federal expense, was more than the Republicans could stand. "The President," Senator Taft protested bitterly, "is blackguarding the Congress at every whistle station in the country." The Democratic Committee immediately wired officials along Truman's route, asking if they agreed with Taft's description of their communities. As might be expected, they emphatically did not. "If Senator Taft referred to Pocatello as 'whistle stop,'" the indignant head of the Idaho town's Chamber of Commerce wired back, "it is apparent that he has not visited progressing Pocatello since time of his father's 1908 campaign for President."

Whatever the Republicans might say about his trip, Truman was highly satisfied. "I had never lost the faith, as some of those around me seemed to," he wrote later, "and I found renewed encouragement and confidence in the response that came from the crowds." In addition, the journey west established the free-swinging style Truman was to use in later campaign trips, and it set up the Republican Congress as his punching bag. But before he squared off against the Republicans, Truman had to overcome elements within his own party that were determined to deny him the nomination.

The idea of running General Dwight D. Eisenhower for President had occurred to the Republicans months before. But in January of 1948, when his admirers appeared to be getting serious, Ike had firmly declared: "I am not available for and could not accept nomination to high political office." That seemed to settle matters—so far as the Republicans were concerned. But some Democrats, in what must surely be a classic example of wishful thinking, concluded that Eisenhower's rejection of politics applied only to Republican politics. Eisenhower had never voted, and no one knew his views on the issues of the day. All this made little difference to the "Eisencrats," who included such strange political bedfellows as liberals James Roosevelt and Chester Bowles, big-city bosses Frank Hague and Jake Arvey, and southern segregationists Richard Russell and Strom Thurmond. They were drawn to Eisenhower simply because they were sure he could win.

But Eisenhower, who was then president of Columbia University, still was not interested in politics. A week before the Democratic convention opened in Philadelphia on July 12, he announced: "I will not at this time identify myself with any political party and could not accept nomination for any political office."

Incredibly enough, some Democrats refused to take even that No for an answer. A measure of their desperation was a proposal by Senator Claude Pepper of Florida that the Democrats draft Eisenhower as a "national" rather than a "party" candidate and let him pick his own running mate and write his own platform. Eisenhower responded with a statement that was the clearest of its kind since General William Tecumseh Sherman turned down the Republicans in 1884: "No matter under what terms, conditions or premises a proposal might be couched, I would refuse to accept the nomination." That was enough, even for Pepper. The dissident liberals now made an attempt to persuade Supreme Court Justice William O. Douglas to accept a draft. When Douglas also declined, the rebels had no choice but to call off their rebellion.

As the Democrats gathered in Philadelphia, the prospects were for a dull and depressing convention. It did not turn out that way. Instead, the Democratic party caught fire in Philadelphia, and the man who struck the first spark was the convention keynoter, Senator Alben Barkley of Kentucky. Barkley, who had been sworn in to the House of Representatives on the day of Woodrow Wilson's first inauguration, remained at seventy one of the party's staunchest bulwarks and one of its most colorful orators. From the moment he mounted the rostrum in Convention Hall to face the delegates, the microphones, and the TV cameras, it was obvious that the old war horse was in rare form. "We have assembled here for a great purpose," the Senator announced. "We are here to give the American people an accounting of our stewardship in the administration of their affairs for sixteen outstanding, eventful years, for not one of which we make an apology."

The delegates, suddenly roused from their lethargy, cheered. But the Senator was only warming up. The Republicans, Barkley noted, proposed "to clean the cobwebs" from the national government. "I am not an expert on cobwebs. But if my memory does not betray me, when the Democratic party took over . . . sixteen years ago, even the spiders were so weak from starvation they could not weave a cobweb in any department of the government in Washington." That brought down the house. And when Barkley concluded his hour-long oration with a call "to lead the children of men . . . into a free world and a free life," the delegates leaped to their feet in a demonstration that lasted more than half an hour.

Barkley's rousing speech not only instilled life into the convention, it also brought about his nomination as Vice President, a development that Truman had neither anticipated nor desired. Truman originally had hoped to bolster the ticket with a youngish New Dealer, and his first choice was fifty-year-old Justice Douglas. But Douglas, who had already refused to be the presidential candidate of the dissident liberals, turned Truman down too. This threw the race for the Vice Presidency wide open, and when Barkley's speech made him the party's hero, Truman had to accept him.

Before the convention closed, Truman's strategy received another jolt. He had hoped he could minimize friction between the southern and northern wings by having the convention adopt a relatively mild platform plank on civil rights. The platform committee went along with the President's wishes, despite the bitter protests of a group of liberals led by Hubert H. Humphrey, the outspoken young mayor of Minneapo-

CONTINUED ON PAGE 104

THE VICTORS

Harry S. Truman, winner of perhaps the biggest political upset in United States history, is greeted the day following the election at Washington's Union Station by his Vice President-elect, Alben Barkley, who was not Truman's choice but who had won nomination on the strength of a dynamic convention keynote speech.

Oh say can you see
Any changes in me?

—OR—

THREE CHEERS FOR THE CHERRY, RINSO

By NORMAN KOTKER

Wake up, America, before it's too late! Rally round the flag while we still have the chance! The threat to Old Glory has never been greater, even in the darkest days of the Republic's history, and even though today the American flag flies—albeit a bit shakily—all around the world. The threat comes not, as you might expect, from a foreign power; it comes from within, for slowly and almost imperceptibly the American flag is changing color, right before our eyes. It's still red, white, and blue, but it's no longer the red, white, and blue that we used to know. The flag I originally pledged my allegiance to had stripes of a crisp but subdued red and a field of fine dark blue. A glance at the flags displayed anywhere around the country—at parades, at schools, at shopping centers, over your alderman's barbecue pit, along Fifth Avenue in New York, or wherever a number of flags fly together—will show that these colors have been transformed into Disneyland or pop-art colors. The blue (which is supposed to stand for loyalty) is often what

the garment district would call electric blue, and sometimes it leaves America altogether to become French blue or even, sad to say, royal blue. The red (for the blood shed by patriots) looks sometimes like a stop light, sometimes like a pizza, sometimes like artificially flavored cherry Jello. Both the red and the blue seem to be more suited to a drum majorette's uniform than to a flag.

What has caused the alarming change in color? Are the flag makers taking undue liberties? No, it's all just part of the march of progress, for nowadays about one in five American flags is made from synthetic fibers like nylon or acrylic, instead of cotton or wool bunting—which is what Betsy Ross used when (if the story is true) she sewed the first flag in 1776.

A flag made of nylon or acrylic—we might call it "Young Glory"—can indeed be attractive. The material is glossy and slick and durable; it reflects light with great brilliance; and the manufacturers are very scientific about it. It is possible to specify exact spectrographic wave lengths for the colors the United States flag is supposed to have. The Color Association of the United States, a quasi-official organization based in New York, has simplified the problem, reducing the specifications to a colorimetric code and assigning a cable number to each color, thus facilitating orders from big textile firms.

The cable numbers of the colors of the United States flag, under this system, are 70180 (Old Glory Red), 70001 (white), and 70075 (Old Glory Blue). They add up to 210,256, a very mystic number which will not be mentioned again. (Americans will be pleased to know that Old Glory Red also appears on the national flags of France and England and even Cuba. The Russian flag is a color called, ironically,

MICHAEL RAMUS

WHITE, AND (POW!) ELECTRIC BLUE!

U.S. Army Scarlet, with the hammer and sickle a shade known as Lemon Yellow.)

But Old Glory Red and Blue are considered absolutely necessary only in flags that are purchased by the government and made in accordance with Federal Specifications DDD-F-416c, a fine, twenty-four-page brochure that is short on poetry but filled with technical drawings and even more technical language. When it comes to flags that are not made for official use, there are no rigid requirements.

Beyond that, however, the synthetic fibers have introduced a new difficulty with which science, so far, is unprepared to cope. It seems that 70180, Old Glory Red, and 70075, Old Glory Blue, strike the eye of the beholder rather differently in nylon or acrylic than they do in good old wool or cotton, since the human mind, irritatingly enough, is more complicated than a spectroscope. They're the same colors, as far as scientific measurement of wave length goes; but, by golly, they don't look the same.

Americans have traditionally been profoundly concerned with the way they treat the flag. The law goes to great and almost tiresome pains to regulate both its display and its proportions. The national ensign is supposed to be hoisted briskly, for instance, and lowered ceremoniously; if anyone should make the mistake of hoisting it ceremoniously and lowering it briskly, he is breaking the law. And according to presidential order, the breadth of the stars should be 6.16 per cent of the entire width of the flag. In this case, the width means the distance from top to bottom, not (as one might expect) from one side to

Mr. Kotker, formerly on the staff of Horizon *magazine, is now an editor with the American Heritage book division.*

the other. The order was issued by President Eisenhower, who is not noted for precision of speech.

Not long ago, when a very enterprising manufacturer of ladies' undergarments tried to market a girdle overprinted with stars and stripes, the Daughters of the American Revolution attacked in force until the unmentionables were withdrawn. What happened to those already sold? They were, one hopes, lowered—with ceremony. But so far nobody has confronted the new threat that Young Glory, or Pop Art Glory, presents to Old Glory. Many hearts may still beat true for the red, white, and blue; but just which red, white, and blue they are beating for is now a moot point. It is to be hoped that we'll still be able not only to see, by the dawn's early light, but to *recognize* what so proudly we hailed, etc. And:

> *May the service, united, ne'er sever,*
> *But hold to their colors so true;*
> *The Army and Navy forever,*
> *Three cheers for the 70180, 70001, and 70075!*

The fearless sailors who manned America's whaling fleet in the nineteenth century were no strangers to danger, but even the bravest trembled at the unknown prospects of becoming

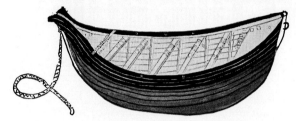

CASTAWAYS ON

A heavy gale had blown up suddenly over the fishing grounds northeast of Japan, and the captain of the whaler *Lawrence,* ten months out of Poughkeepsie, New York, was in a dilemma. Should he cut loose the whale alongside and sail out the storm, or try to save his valuable prize by letting the ship float with the current? Yankee frugality triumphed; the decision cost Captain Baker his ship and his life.

An hour or so before midnight on May 27, 1846, the drifting *Lawrence* grounded, rolled on her starboard side, and bilged. Baker quickly launched his whaleboat and, pulling away into the darkness with a handful of the crew, shouted back through the wind, "Each man for himself." He was never seen again. Nor was the first mate, Mr. Myers, whose boat slipped its bow tackle, plunged into the sea, and was stove to pieces. Only the boat commanded by the second mate, George Howe, survived. Getting safely away from the ship proved to be the easiest part of the trip home.

Of the various hazards American whalemen faced in the mid-nineteenth century, perhaps the most frightening was to be cast up on the forbidding shores of feudal Japan. Since 1638, when that nation's rulers became convinced that Christianity, disseminated by European missionaries, was a monstrous foreign plot to seize control of their islands, Japan was off limits to outsiders, upon pain of death. Threatening laws to the contrary, foreign shipping in Japanese waters gradually increased. During the first part of the nineteenth century, vessels flying the colors of an expansionist young nation, the United States, began to appear in growing numbers.

In 1842, the Tokugawa shogunate, which ruled Japan in the name of the impotent emperors, became alarmed at the trouncing just administered to a Chinese fleet by the British in the so-called Opium War. Accordingly, the shoguns relaxed their decree of *Ni-nen-naku,* or "no second thought": henceforth, instead

of killing castaways, local officials were to give the intruders water and food so that they might quickly sail away.

Howe and his six crewmates were well aware of the danger that awaited them on land, but they had no choice. Their provisions were exhausted by the second day; their small boat was being buffeted constantly, and a driving snow aggravated the misery of the ill-clad seamen. On June 3, Howe steered the boat into a protected bay, where the men caught a seal and enjoyed their first meal in four days.

Afterward, Howe and five of his men hiked inland about a mile, but they found no one and returned to the beach at dusk. The man left at the boat reported a visit by two Orientals, who, upon learning through sign language the number of *Lawrence* survivors, had fled in terror. What happened next typified the ambivalent character of feudal Japan, which was unwilling to accommodate the outside world and yet unable to prevent its intrusion, undecided whether to kill its uninvited guests or to pamper them with exotic delicacies. Howe later wrote:

The next morning we got into the boat and steered for the mouth of a river on one side of the bay. As we approached it we saw what appeared to us to be a fort with spears glistening in the sun above the walls; but on coming nearer, we found it was a piece of cloth extended about three quarters of a mile, and painted so as to represent a fort with guns. Here, as we landed, about sixty men, armed with swords and spears, ran towards us and motioned us to go away. We however continued approaching them until we got very near, when we all fell on our knees before them. One of them came up to me, and would have struck me down with his sword, but his hand was held back by an old man. . . . I made signs to them that we were harmless people, and wanted food. After much talking among themselves they brought us some rice and fish, which we ate. They then again motioned us to be off.

The problem, as Howe tried to explain, was logis-

FORBIDDEN SHORES

By ROBERT S. GALLAGHER

tical. The whaleboat was too small for an extended sea voyage. East and West stared at each other in dismay: the Americans wanted to go but could not; the Japanese, forbidden to build seagoing vessels, could neither force nor assist their visitors to depart. What ensued was seventeen months of uneasy captivity, considered by the seamen as a period of horrendous cruelty, and by their hosts as an unwelcome test of informal diplomacy. Both viewpoints had some validity.

Japan was a closed society, but it was not without egress. At Nagasaki, the Dutch, in reward for their help in suppressing a revolt by Christian peasants in 1637, maintained a trading preserve on the tiny island of Deshima. Once a year a Dutch ship called there, and just as frequently the Dutch envoy or *opperhoofd* was granted an audience by the shoguns at Edo (modern Tokyo). Whatever business Japan conducted with the West was done through the Dutch at Deshima. Increasingly, this business involved the return of "waifs," or shipwrecked sailors, who, if the Japanese decided that they were not missionaries, would be repatriated by the Dutch on their ship to Java.

The *Lawrence* survivors had not come to preach. They did not, in fact, know where they were, and it was only later they learned they had landed on Etorofu, an island in the Kurile chain. Nevertheless, for the next eleven months, Howe and his men were interrogated daily—about their country, their religion, and the circumstances of their arrival. A government artist, Ryuzaemon Yoshida, was brought in to record every detail of their physical appearance—tattoos, moles, pockmarks, and hair and eye coloring. (His water colors—now in the possession of Carl H. Boehringer, executive director of the American Chamber of Commerce in Japan and a long-time resident there—are reproduced on these pages.) Howe and his mates were alternately cajoled by minor officials and maltreated by xenophobic guards, "who frequently struck us, and insulted us." Howe remembered one

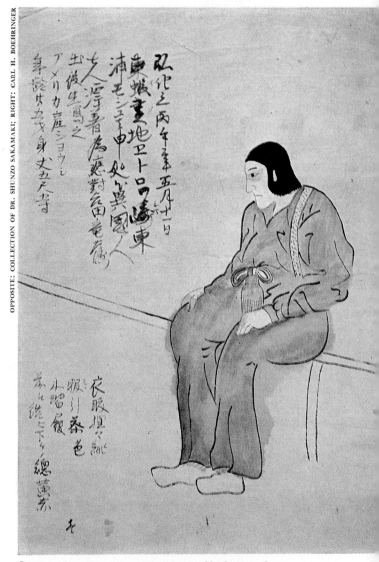

SHOSHI, 25 YEARS OLD; 5 SHAKU 5 SUN [65.6 INCHES] TALL; SHIRT CRIMSON RED; TROUSERS BROWN; WOODEN SHOES.

Second Mate George Howe was so described by the artist, whose work (including the stylized whaleboat opposite) is considered the earliest Japanese attempt at portraying Americans.

Hyo, an American, 25 years old, 6 shaku 5 bu [72.2 inches] tall; shirt is light blue with stripes; trousers gray.

Probably Peter Williams, 24, of Boston.

Maihei, aged 18, 5 shaku 8 sun [69.2 inches] tall; wearing a light blue striped shirt; trousers gray.

Henry Spencer, 21, of Harrison [N.J.?].

Marui, from America; 18 years old; 5 shaku 3 sun [63.2 inches] tall; shirt is orange in color; trousers gray.

Probably Murphy Wells, 19, no address.

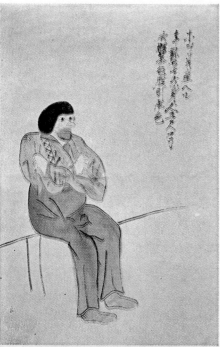

Heru, 27 years old; 5 shaku 4 sun [64.4 inches] tall; shirt is brown; trousers are gray; he comes from Hosoki.

Known only as Bill, 27, of New York.

Sho, 35 years old; 5 shaku 2 sun [62 inches] tall; shirt is purple in color; trousers reddish in color with stripes.

Known only as Joe, 39, of New York.

Tehe, 28; 5 shaku 5 sun [65.6 inches] tall; tattooed all over body; blue shirt.

This man, whose English name is unknown, was murdered after attempting to escape.

occasion when they were plied with "sukee," then questioned again by their jailers, "thinking perhaps that under the influence of the liquor we would give them whatever information we had before endeavored to suppress."

The transcripts of the interminable interviews were forwarded with the water colors to the district governor, who, after conferring with his superiors, ordered the waifs shipped to Nagasaki. Howe reported:

They put us on board of a junk and stowed us all in the hold, a dark, filthy place, and during the time we were in her, some three or four months, not a single moment were we allowed to step on deck to breath the fresh air or see the light. One day we were made to wash ourselves, and clean clothes were given us, and we were conducted into the cabin, which was beautifully fitted up with silk and gold ornaments; they then gave us each a carpet to sit upon, and made us understand that [the emperor's son] was coming on board to see us. By-and-by we heard a great stir outside, and all the people fell on their faces to the ground, and we were made to do the same.

The prince questioned them for an hour through a Japanese linguist who spoke a little Dutch, and that evening the prisoners received a royal gift of a box of sweetmeats. Then Howe and his men were thrust back into the hold, where again they were at the mercy of their guards.

At Nagasaki, the seamen were carried through the streets in wooden cages to the town hall, where the questioning was resumed. First they were required—at sword's point—to trample and spit upon a print of the crucifixion; then they were shown epaulettes from the British and American navies and asked to point to the kind worn in their own country. One afternoon, they were surprised to see a European sitting among the Japanese judges; they were more amazed when this gentleman, confident that only they would understand, said simply: "If there are any John Bulls among you, you had better not say anything about it." The speaker was the Dutch *opperhoofd*, Joseph Henrij Levyssohn, whom the Nagasaki officials frequently pressed into service as an interpreter.

A few days after this crucial interview, one of the men, ignoring the warnings of his shipmates, tried to escape and was, according to Howe, "inhumanly murdered by the Japanese." The Japanese insisted that the sailor died of dysentery, a version corroborated by Levyssohn; but under the circumstances, Howe's account carries more authority.

Shortly after this unfortunate incident, the six remaining survivors of the *Lawrence*'s twenty-three-man crew were paroled in the custody of Levyssohn, who ten days later put them aboard the Dutch ship *Hertogenbosch,* bound for Batavia. There the U.S. consul

"extended his protection towards us," Howe wrote, "and furnished us with the few articles of clothing we were so much in need of."

Howe's description of his experiences from shipwreck to repatriation first appeared in a letter to the Singapore *Free Press* on January 6, 1848. A copy of the article was promptly dispatched to Secretary of State (and future President) James Buchanan by Dr. Peter Parker, secretary to the American legation in Canton, China. Parker noted that the *Lawrence* survivors were being held incommunicado at the very time when Commodore James Biddle, with two American warships, was in Tokyo Bay trying unsuccessfully to negotiate a treaty with the shoguns. Parker added prophetically:

The fate of the "Lawrence" and her men is probably but one of many similar catastrophies, with this difference, that none of the others were so fortunate as to return to narrate their sufferings at the hands of the cruel inhabitants of the "land of the rising sun," and doubtless it will be considered by the government of the United States as a new argument and a fair pretext for repeating an embassy to Japan as soon as convenient and practicable.

It was. When Commodore Matthew C. Perry sailed his black-hulled fleet on its famous mission to Japan in 1853, he carried with him elaborate instructions from the Secretary of the Navy that specifically cited the wreck of the *Lawrence* and the "great barbarity" her crew had suffered. Perry was sent to conclude a treaty with Japan that would insure, in President Millard Fillmore's phrase, "friendship, amity, and intercourse" between the two nations—meaning coaling stations for U.S. ships and trade agreements for U.S. merchants. But the first stated aim of the proposed treaty was to provide humane treatment for shipwrecked Americans. And should persuasion fail, the State Department told Perry, he was to inform the Japanese "that if any acts of cruelty should hereafter be practised upon citizens of this country, whether by the government or by the inhabitants of Japan, they will be severely chastised." Perry found that the intimation of force was enough; forts painted on silk curtains were no match for Yankee armament. The treaty he concluded in 1854 assured decent treatment for shipwrecked sailors; the ports of Shimoda and Hakodate were designated for provisioning American ships; and, within a few years, Japan was at last opened for commercial exploitation.

The editors wish to express their appreciation to Mr. Boehringer, whose initial discovery of the Lawrence *portraits in a Tokyo print shop and subsequent research on the shipwreck made this article possible; and to Dr. Shunzo Sakamaki, of the University of Hawaii, for his technical assistance.*

When the movie version of *Lord Jim* was released a few years ago, it had a special interest for me because a friend of mine, an Englishman, had been a member of the film crew that spent several months on location in Cambodia. After I saw the finished product, with its awe-inspiring scenes of some of the world's most inhospitable terrain, I remembered my friend's reply when I asked about the hardships he had encountered.

"Hardships!" he laughed. "We lived better down there than we ever did in London. All the luxuries. If we wanted anything, a jet could fetch it from anywhere in the world within hours."

He explained that location shooting off the beaten track had become a perfected routine, learned from the experience of earlier companies—"from movies like *The African Queen, Lawrence of Arabia,* and

Surviving encounters with an awesome variety of enraged wildlife—rhinos, lions, tsetse flies, studio brass—Trader Horn, *Hollywood's first jungle spectacular, became the progenitor of hundreds of white-hunter-meets-white-goddess epics*

Damn the Crocodiles—

KEEP THE CAMERAS ROLLING!

By BYRON RIGGAN

King Solomon's Mines. And, of course, they owed a great deal to the pioneering expeditions—particularly to the granddaddy of them all, *Trader Horn.* Now, making *that* film was really an undertaking."

Trader Horn! Through the fog of memory floated a flickering image of a pale young woman with waist-length ash-blonde hair; scantily clad, she stands in a jungle clearing surrounded by a mob of nearly naked and highly agitated natives. I also recalled a giant billboard advertisment showing the girl flanked by a handsome young man in a pith helmet and an older man in a floppy khaki hat. The jungle looms behind them, and they are frozen in attitudes of acute anxiety as they stare off-camera toward some approaching peril. Then I remembered some of the rumors that have followed *Trader Horn* down through the years, rumors nearly as weird as anything depicted in the film itself: that the young actress contracted a deadly African disease and slowly expired in a Hollywood nursing home; that the leading man gave up civilization and retired to the jungle; and that some of the natives employed in the film later became organizers of the Mau Mau. A passion for jungle films and a re-awakened curiosity about all those stories needed only my friend's remarks to set me looking into the history of *Trader Horn.*

On a January night in 1931, a noisy and titillated throng surged around Grauman's Chinese Theatre in Hollywood. The occasion was the most glittering and glamorous film opening the world had yet seen. *Trader Horn* was a landmark in movie history: it was not only the first "talkie" made by Metro-Goldwyn-Mayer, but the first ever made outside the United States by any Hollywood company. It had cost a record $2,900,000 and had been two years in preparation; one of those years had been spent in what the press agents liked to call "the dark heart of Africa."

Limousines purred up to the theatre entrance and discharged the movie idols of the day. Sleekly tailored actors and actresses in furs and feathers advanced, with alligator smiles for the crowd of screaming fans. Above the pandemonium, searchlights alerted the heavens.

The film's romantic leads, Edwina Booth and Duncan Renaldo, arrived arm in arm, beaming. Miss Booth was a blonde, twenty-one-year-old Mormon from Provo, Utah. Except for an earlier bit part, this was her first film. Tragically, it was also her last starring role. Duncan Renaldo (real name, Renaldo Duncan) was a handsome half-Spanish, half-Scottish orphan who had been raised in France.

The third and best-known star of the picture was Harry Carey, a former New York law student who, with his characteristic shy grin, had become a talented

M.G.M.

and respected actor. He and his wife, Olive, were not at Grauman's that night; they were in New York, where they attended a simultaneous opening with Mayor Jimmy Walker.

The film—shakily based on the 1927 best seller *Trader Horn,* written by a white hunter named Alfred Aloysius Horn (and edited by Ethelreda Lewis, an English novelist)—was a story of heroic quest. A young and wealthy South American named Peru is on safari with Horn. They become involved in a search for a missionary's daughter kidnapped as a child by a native tribe. Because of her extreme blondeness, she has been kept by the tribe as their fetish and goddess. The story tells of the perils that beset the two men as they search for and finally (of course) rescue the girl.

The picture's press agents continually insisted that nothing about this movie was fake, that everything in it actually happened. And for once the ballyhoo was not far from the truth. "Sometimes you cannot believe your eyes," said a review in *Theatre Magazine.* "You cannot believe that human flesh went through this and came out whole. Well, it has. Thrilling, beautiful, incredibly yet utterly veracious record of a forbidden and inhospitable world." Commented the *Literary Digest:* "Director W. S. Van Dyke has brought back from the African jungles a series of audible-film incidents which for sheer thrills and undiluted realism have never been surpassed."

The film's initial hoop-la faded predictably; perhaps just as inevitably, in those subsequent years, several members of the expedition died, including director Van Dyke, who had written a book about the making of the picture entitled *Horning Into Africa.* The only survivors, as far as I could learn from M.G.M., were Duncan Renaldo and Harry Carey's widow, Olive, who unknowingly lived within a few miles of each other in southern California, and both agreed to interviews.

Renaldo met me at the Santa Barbara airport. Now in his middle sixties, he still shows, in his aquiline features and piercing eyes, traces of the matinee idol. He drove me out to his ranch house, where my attention was at once attracted by two large oils of a Masai chief and his wife, painted by the actor himself. An African spirit drum and a dozen other mementos of the expedition were crowded into the living room and dining room. "As you see," he said, "that movie was one of the great experiences of my life."

Later we went to see Olive Carey, who greeted us cheerily, embracing Renaldo with cries of delight. Talk soon turned to the film.

Horn's book had been bought by M.G.M.'s Irving Thalberg, who thought it would make a spectacular movie. But how could a mobile village of film makers sustain life in a little-known and dangerous part of the world? And what about casting? Obviously, to live in close association for a long period in rough country would require of all hands courage, character, intelligence, and tact.

The choice of romantic lead was easy. Renaldo was an outdoor man with spirit, virile looks, and acting experience. Carey was the studio's first choice to play the role of Horn, but he did not fancy such a long trip away from his family. He took the part only after Thalberg agreed to give his wife a small role and to permit him to take their two children as far as Nairobi; there they could attend school and their parents could visit them.

The difficult role to fill was that of the White Goddess. She had to be blonde and beautiful. She had to be fiery and imperious, yet capable of projecting an innocent wood-sprite quality when confronted by the sophisticated white men. "In other words," said Renaldo, "she had to be the most exotic personality possible."

Thalberg considered the entire crop of M.G.M. female stars. Bessie Love, hoping to be chosen, dyed her hair ash-blonde. Thelma Todd was tested, and Thalberg even thought of Jeanette MacDonald. After all, a blonde fetish might be even more irresistible if she could sing.

Then one day a young starlet marched into the administrative offices of M.G.M. and demanded to be paid for posing for stills—a job that starlets, and even stars, traditionally did for nothing. "I won't do it for nothing," declared Edwina Booth. "It took up my time and I want to be paid." Thalberg liked her spirit and energy, and Miss Booth was scheduled for a test.

Renaldo recalled that during the run-through for the test "the change that came over this rather demure little girl was extraordinary. She displayed a highly volatile temperament that was perfect for the role of the Goddess. The crew burst into applause and she was hired on the spot. The test was never filmed."

For director, Thalberg picked W. S. Van Dyke, who had already shown a great talent for nature films. Van Dyke was entranced with the job; "It was the most exciting project of my life," he told friends afterward. For many in the troupe, it was nearly the last project of their lives.

It all began luxuriously enough on the *Ile de France* in New York Harbor. "We sailed around ten at night," Renaldo related, "and as soon as we were in the open sea, they opened the bar. From that moment on, the ship was a floating cabaret." Those ladies and gentlemen of the Prohibition era bellied up to the bar with enthusiasms that often exceeded their capacities. "I

Trader Horn *called for only one white goddess, and Edwina Booth, nearest the camera in the picture at top left, won the role. Scores of Pygmies were needed, however, and most of those in the adjacent photo made it onto celluloid. Above, Miss Booth relaxes in her alfresco on-location dressing room. In the picture at right center, Harry Carey, out on a limb, surveys the crocodile-infested waters that will figure in an upcoming scene. At the near right, actors and crew are perched above Murchison Falls.*

have never seen so many drunk people in my life," said Olive Carey.

Edwina Booth, with her strong religious principles, stayed aloof from all that. But, Renaldo remembered, "Everyone had eyes for her—including me. Her features were almost perfect, and she had a very ingratiating voice. She was one of the most levelheaded women I've ever known. Her morals and standards of conduct were very strict."

To Olive, "Edwina was a very high-minded and intelligent young woman. She was interested in life and took it very seriously."

The late John McClain, then a press agent with the expedition and subsequently a syndicated columnist, had told me on the telephone: "She was a pleasant enough woman, pretty, but frankly I thought she was a bit of a bore. She was such a proper do-gooder. I don't think she had much sense of humor."

In any case, movie stars in those days had an aura of glamour that surpasses anything seen today. Renaldo fought off women who tried to get into his stateroom, while Edwina had to fight off the men, particularly a fellow passenger named Jean Borotra, a French tennis ace. "He kept kissing her hand," Renaldo recalled, "and the kisses kept getting longer and more frequent. Finally, one night Harry Carey came to Edwina's rescue and kicked him in the backside. This provoked a challenge for a duel and the captain had to intervene."

When the ship reached Le Havre, the film unit disembarked early in the morning and was ushered into a nearby shed for some publicity shots. In those days magnesium flares were used for taking pictures. The shed had recently been used to store some kind of volatile material, and when the hung-over, bleary, jittery members of the company bared their teeth for pictures, the magnesium went off and the resultant explosion blew out the sides of the shed and blackened the faces and clothes of the stunned movie makers. In a daze, they were assisted from the building just before the roof collapsed. Unaccountably, no one was hurt.

In Paris, Van Dyke and Renaldo went to see the sights. At Napoleon's tomb, Van Dyke stood for a long time looking down on the emperor. "When we went out," Renaldo remembered, "I noticed that Van Dyke had tucked his right hand into his coat and over his heart. At that moment, I think, he changed into a general. From then on the members of the unit began receiving morning notices like 'Henceforward the troupe will move en masse' and 'Exactly at such and such a time we rendezvous.'"

The troupe moved en masse by train to Genoa, where it embarked on the freighter *Usaramo* bound for Mombasa, Kenya.

A few days south of Arabia, Van Dyke instructed Edwina to go on the sun deck to accustom herself to tropical sunlight. She did this for several days, but one afternoon she suddenly went white and fainted. The next morning she was up and in good spirits, so no one thought any more about it. The voyage continued down a serene Indian Ocean toward Mombasa.

But the world they had left behind was anything but serene: Van Dyke found frantic cables awaiting him when the *Usaramo* docked at Mombasa in March of 1929. Because Al Jolson had been heard as well as seen in *The Jazz Singer*, M.G.M. now wanted *Trader Horn* to be done with sound.

The first sound truck to arrive fell from a broken crane into Mombasa Harbor. There were more cables and more worry, but at last the company had three sound trucks. Meanwhile, the main group climbed aboard a narrow-gauge railway train and set off for Nairobi, where the production's safari was to be formed.

The *Trader Horn* expedition was one of the largest safaris ever mounted, surpassing even that of Edward, Prince of Wales, a few years before. There were thirty-five white people, two hundred natives, ten Buick and Chevrolet pickup trucks, the three sound trucks, sixteen cameras with their replacement parts, and all the laboratory equipment for developing and printing film. There were also toiletries, clothes, medical supplies, liquor, canned foods, reflectors, generators for refrigeration (to keep the film—not the food—cool). Each white person was assigned a bearer who did everything from making the bed to giving a bath. Food was mainly canned; meat was shot on the hoof as the party went along.

In late April all was ready, and the party took off into the bush. On the first night everyone went to bed early, but as deep night fell and the bush came alive with mysterious growls and shrieks, Edwina, Harry and Olive, Renaldo, and Van Dyke crept from their tents and gathered about the large campfire. All but the teetotalling leading lady drank Johnny Walker Scotch or Old Pensioner gin, listening to the wail of the hyenas and the occasional blare of an elephant. In *Horning Into Africa*, Van Dyke remembered that first night and wondered if the others had shared with him the deep and atavistic fear: "Will I be eaten by wild animals?"

But they grew accustomed to the jungle, and camp life quickly became routine. The day began at six, when one's "boy" entered, carrying a cup of coffee or tea. The group ate breakfast together in the mess tent, where the orders of the day were handed out.

M.G.M.

CULVER

CULVER

COLLECTION OF DUNCAN RENALDO

These pictures, in a zigzag pattern from the top, pretty well sum up the story line of Hollywood's first great jungle movie. Peru (Duncan Renaldo) and Trader Horn (Harry Carey) interrupt their safari to take up the search for the White Goddess ... they find her just before they are captured by natives and held for ceremonial killing ... she helps them escape ... after first killing a guard ... because she has fallen in love with Peru ... who persuades her to sail with him to civilization.... The end.

M.G.M.

CULVER

There was no detailed script. Everyone knew the story: Peru and Trader Horn, travelling through the jungle, meet the mother (Olive) of the kidnapped girl. She tells them she is going to a native village where she believes her daughter is being held prisoner. Later the two men discover that the mother has been murdered by natives, and they decide to take up the search. They are captured and prepared for ceremonial killing. But the Goddess appears, falls in love with Peru, and ultimately helps them escape. There is a long sequence as they flee, carrying the girl with them. This skeletal story was fleshed out with dialogue made up by the actors and Van Dyke as they went along, depending on what befell them. Sometimes it was encounters with crocodiles and lions, other times with elephants and snakes.

Of Van Dyke's direction, Renaldo recalled: "He was brusque, but he was marvelous with the natives. At times we would have scenes with a thousand of them that he had rounded up from the bush. We never did our scenes more than twice. He thought this gave the best feeling of naturalness, which was, after all, what we wanted to convey. Most of us were not acting, but just reacting to actual happenings. After all, when a herd of elephants charged us we didn't have a chance for retakes."

As the days wore on, Van Dyke's direction became more imperious and the morning notices more peremptory: "Natives at night must be dressed in white and carry lanterns." "When attacked by a native, don't hit him on the head, kick him in the shins. He is more sensitive there."

Van Dyke planned to use Murchison Falls, in Uganda, as a base camp for three months. When Ugandan officials, fearing the company's exposure to the tsetse fly, said they would "not permit one man, woman, child or animal to go up into that district from this colony," Van Dyke replied that neither the whites nor the natives were from Uganda. And that was that.

Van Dyke later wrote: "You couldn't suppose that anyone would be damn fool enough to go up into such a place after such a warning, would you? It gave me a pause . . . yet there were the hippos, there were the crocs, and there were the falls, and in no other place in Africa were there so many . . . nor such beautiful falls. There was no one to whom I could turn for advice. The responsibility must rest squarely on my shoulders. Maybe it was the heat. I had already had a fairly rotten case of malaria but anyway, perfectly insane, I decided to go, explained the circumstances to the people, and they decided to go with me."

Murchison Falls is located north of Lake Albert, where the Victoria Nile plunges down a 120-foot drop. The noise is horrendous, the sight unnerving. "Somehow [it] reminds me of Dante's Inferno," wrote Van Dyke. "The chasm and the falls are seething cauldrons in which it is impossible for any fish in the world to live. And that is more or less the secret of the fat crocs. They lie in wait at the foot of the falls and eat the fish that are swept down and killed in the passage."

Renaldo recounted that for three months they camped on one of the most spectacular sites in the world:

The Nile is one thousand feet wide at that point and crammed with crocodiles and hippos. There is no kind of creation that isn't represented in the water, or above the ground. Life is teeming so much that you can actually hear it in the water. If you take a glass of water from the Nile and boil it down, you will have about a quarter of it left as residual animal life of the most fantastic variety imaginable. But in order to live there, everything has to eat something else, and you hear this agony going on night and day.

The crocodiles were immense beasts like prehistoric monsters, twenty feet long, four feet wide at the shoulders. Edwina and I would sit outside our tents at night and watch a flotilla of crocodiles sliding up to the bank. All you can see is their eyes, great knobs protruding above the water. At night if there is any light at all, they shine red as the beasts move upstream so smoothly they leave no ripples.

Sometimes the hippos would come snorting and stumbling into our camp and sometimes go lumbering off dragging ropes and tents.

And then there were the bugs. Scorpions got into boots despite all precautions. Flying ants would dive right through mosquito netting. "You couldn't eat soup," said Renaldo, "because a thousand insects would commit suicide in your spoon. We had insects in our eyebrows and our hair and we found ticks on our bodies for weeks afterwards. This was a terrible time for Edwina with her long hair."

Van Dyke wrote: "Frequently, in the dead of night, I would hear a wild yell and wake up to see some member of my company flying out of his camp absolutely nude, slapping and rubbing every part of his anatomy. He had innocently pitched his tent in front of an ant safari, and when these ants take it into their heads to come into your camp, you might just as well move out until the parade is over. No one ever stopped to think of clothing. If it were a man's yell we heard, some of us would sometimes go to his assistance; if it were one of the women who was yelling, we would politely cover our heads and let her take care of herself—oh yeah?"

Van Dyke's diary shows entries like: "June 6. Roberts [a cameraman] suffering terribly from tsetse fly bites. Neck swollen terribly. Miss Booth hit with sun."

CONTINUED ON PAGE 100

The men chatting above are Alfred Aloysius Horn, left, author of the book on which Trader Horn was based, and Cecil B. DeMille, who came on at the start of the opening reel to vouch for the production's authenticity. At right, director W. S. Van Dyke stands in his memento-filled Hollywood living room. The other photographs are classics of the publicity genre: the romantic leads drawing romantic beads on each other, the stars on the homeward-bound ship, and the White Goddess on leopard skin.

The period between the First and Second World Wars was, for the Rockies, a time of cruel suspension and uncertain change. Not even we children could pull the covers over our heads and pretend that the bogeymen were not there, for we were surrounded with the wreckage of hopes that once had blossomed as brightly as our own.

The most graphic of the ruins lay in Colorado's Red Mountain district, a six-mile sprawl of abandoned workings along one of the headwater streams of the Uncompahgre River. By horseback across the intervening high ridges, Red Mountain was not far from Telluride, where I lived, but by car it was a long drive around through Ouray and up the resounding Uncompahgre Gorge. Occasionally my stepfather would go there to examine moribund mining claims in which he held an interest, and the trip gave my brother and me and perhaps a friend or two an opportunity to scamper off along the weed-grown bed of the silent narrow-gauge railway for an hour of delicious prowling amidst acres of junk.

Laced among lifeless cabins were long dumps of waste rock, running like petrified tongues from the mouths of the deserted mines that the railroad had once served. Weighted down by each winter's heavy snowfall, the mill and mine buildings, the stores, the little bell-towered church—everything—leaned a little more perilously each year, until one summer we returned to find that another landmark had collapsed into a heap of splintered boards.

We never found much inside the cabins except broken-handled implements, cracked dishes, and oddments of homemade furniture, for the departing residents had removed whatever was usable. Now and then among the waterlogged layers of newspaper that had been tacked to the walls for insulation we would notice a section of print that was still legible, and we would read, without much interest, of what had been happening down in Silverton in 1906. We investigated the wooden snowsheds that led from each house to its privy. We stirred our shoe toes through the

heaps of crumbling tin cans outside the kitchen doors and occasionally saw, without being aware of their value as collectors' items, old whiskey and catsup bottles whose glass had been stained a delicate purple by years of sunshine. Then we'd hear my stepfather honking the car horn and we'd scurry back. We sensed vaguely that we had brushed across lost dreams, and after we returned to Telluride we realized, during uneasy moments, that the stuff of our own lives was slipping away just as inexorably.

For we could detect the grim note that came into the voices of our elders when they mentioned that another mine up in Marshall Basin had closed. We stood around with our mothers while they watched the neighbors across the street move away, leaving behind a For Sale sign that no one ever lifted from the desiccated lawn. Then another, and another, and pretty soon one of the groceries on Colorado Avenue closed, and after that the lace curtains disappeared from the windows of one of the huts, called cribs, down on Pacific Avenue, "the line" where the prostitutes lived.

By August, 1929, the Bank of Telluride was insolvent and the examiners were on the way in. At that point the bank's president, Charles Delos Waggoner, had an inspiration. By a dizzy manipulation of cashiers' checks drawn on the Chase National Bank in New York, he paid off his own bank's obligations and headed for western Canada, half a breath before the alarm was sounded.

Telluride's only benefit was a brief lift in spirit. One of their backcountry boys had outfoxed the city slickers, and for a time the name of their town was on the front page of every major newspaper in the land. In the end, though, Waggoner was caught; he went to prison and the doors of his bank never reopened.

By the beginning of the 1930's the *brump* of the stamp mills above the town had ended, and no amount of shouting could drive the silence away. Those who were left in the town tried. After all, Telluride was the county seat and a certain amount

THE PURPLE MOUNTAINS' FADING MAJESTY

The plundering miners have been replaced by the plundering tourists.

of county business, financed by taxes on the railroad and on the neighboring cattle and sheep ranches, had to go on until mining came back. All over the Rockies people were chanting that litany, which no doubt the inhabitants of Red Mountain had once chanted too: "Mining will come back."

We leaned on frail reeds while we waited. A brief upswing in livestock prices ended in 1927 and the market resumed its long postwar slide into the Depression. Desperate for revenue, many cattlemen took to crowding their animals onto smaller areas and renting the balance of their land to sheep growers. Equally desperate for revenue, the sheepmen let their herds crop to the roots both the rented forage and the grass on the public domain, reducing the range's carrying capacity and creating, with the cattlemen's help, serious problems of erosion.

The rangeland crisis in the mountains was intensified by the same fierce drought that during the early thirties turned the high plains east of the Rockies into dust bowls. Spurred by the disaster, Congress passed the Taylor Grazing Act—named for Edward Taylor, a long-time congressman from western Colorado—thereby placing federal controls over whatever public domain still lay outside of the national forests and national parks. Henceforth the most vital single factor in the swift spread of the American frontier—free land—was no longer available. Men could use the nation's natural resources only under the supervision of gigantic federal bureaus.

The mountain railroads were no better off than the Depression-harried stockmen. All the lines had emerged from the First World War in debt; some were in receivership. The wretched physical condition of Colorado's principal mountain road, the Denver & Rio Grande Western, led jokesters to scoff that its initials really meant Dangerous & Rapidly Growing Worse.

The matter was no joke to the Rio Grande, however, or to its Ridgway-Telluride-Durango subsidiary, the Rio Grande Southern. The company earnestly wanted to abandon the profitless, snow-heaped, flood-tormented narrow-gauge branches and concentrate on improving and shortening its main line between Denver and Salt Lake City. Heeding the howls of local

businessmen who preferred a poor road to none, the Interstate Commerce Commission refused permission. Wretched compromises resulted. Although livestock and ore trains still ran into Telluride and on to Durango more or less as needed, passengers and mail were relegated to a hybrid called the Galloping Goose, a truck body mounted on railroad wheels. There were seats up front for five or six passengers (if that many should ever appear), a van-type body behind for miscellaneous freight, a cowcatcher for nostalgia, and gasoline for power. This unnatural offspring of an efficiency expert's mating with a balance sheet careened along the rusty rails until 1951, when the D. & R.G.W. at last began to abandon its narrow-gauges.

Strangely enough, the Depression that was suffocating the stockmen and the railroads brought a flutter back to the mining industry. Most of the large gold and silver properties in the mountains were controlled by absentee corporations whose directors seldom had either the opportunity or the inclination to sniff around the edges of the cold workings in quest of crumbs. But local men did. Wages were down, materials were cheap, and they hoped that they could dismantle the old mill and mine buildings and make a precarious profit by wringing gold dust out of the tons of debris that had accumulated during the years. For this privilege they paid the owners a royalty, so that no one lost too much in case of failure. Other men, backed by slightly more capital, poked inside the hollowed mountains, found pillars of ore that had not been removed by owners intent on bigger game, and secured royalty leases on those.

These clean-up operations were quickened in 1934 by President Roosevelt's abrupt devaluation of the dollar. Overnight the price of an ounce of gold leaped from $20.67 to $35. Lessees promptly intensified their

CONTINUED ON PAGE 91

OVERLEAF: The majestic mountains are still there, if you can find them for the people swarming over them. On the following two pages, Michael Ramus summarizes the scene in a picture drawn especially for AMERICAN HERITAGE. In the welter of newness, be sure not to miss the old. It is symbolized in the upper right corner by the retreating miner and the defeated dance-hall girl sadly taking her wares elsewhere.

Can the Rockies survive this new invasion? BY DAVID LAVENDER

Was the dead man by the campfire the heavily insured John Hillmon, the unemployed Frederick Walters, or an unknown drifter? The United States Supreme Court pondered . . .

Description of JOHN H. HILLMON at or about the time of disappearance, 1879

◦◦⚬◦◦

AGE—About 37 years of age, 5 feet 9 inches, well built, broad shoulders, erect and weighed 140 to 150 pounds.

HAIR—Dark or brown, when worn long curls upward or outward.

FOREHEAD — Broad, broader through temples than at cheek bones.

EYES—Either dark gray or hazel; very bright, intelligent and well separated.

NOSE—Prominent and slightly Roman, faint scar on bridge which shows white when he laughs, end of nose tipped very slightly to the right.

BEARD—Has worn full beard, but prefers moustache and imperial, is of light brown, several shades lighter than hair. Moustache of medium thickness and length and worn hanging over mouth.

MOUTH—Medium size, with under lip drooping slightly.

TEETH — Prominent when he laughs, with left upper incisor missing or black, probably missing. Teeth may now (1889) be generally defective.

HANDS—Medium size and shapely with long fingers.

FEET—Very proud of his feet, which are small, wears a No. 7 fine boot easily, heavy boots No. 8 probably.

LIMBS—Long, body short in proportion.

SCARS—Ugly scar on right hand (or left), at base of thumb, extending along thick of thumb through crotch and over on upper side, wide as though made by burn or brand. It is the result of a tearing injury and not clean cut. Small scar on back of head on a line with top of left ear, about an inch long. Cut shoe, hair must be it.

Frederick A. Walters

John W. Hillmon

The body in the coffin, said the insurance companies, was probably that of Frederick A. Walters—certainly not that of John W. Hillmon, whose description they ardently circulated in the hope that someone would find him alive. As a matter of policy, Mrs. Hillmon had reasons to hope otherwise.

By BROOKS W. MACCRACKEN

THE CASE OF THE *Anonymous Corpse*

Among *causes célèbres* the Hillmon case is unique; it was not a criminal case and no famous or notorious persons were involved. Murder may —or may not—have been done, but there was no murder trial. It was only a young woman's suit against three life insurance companies, the question being whether she was or was not a widow. Yet it was a political and legal storm center for nearly a quarter of a century, from before the assassination of Garfield until after the assassination of McKinley. It coincided with the rise of the Grangers and the Populists and the coming of the trust busters; and for all of them it was a ready-made and graphic story of the constant struggle of the little people against the forces of big business.

The case began in 1878, at Lawrence, Kansas. John W. Hillmon, aged thirty-three, was a roving cattle herder without visible property or means, currently resident in Lawrence. His most valuable asset was the friendship of Levi Baldwin, who was known in Lawrence as a cattleman with money. In the fall of 1878, Hillmon cemented this friendship by marrying Baldwin's cousin Sallie Quinn, a pleasant and popular waitress. Bride and groom set up light housekeeping in a room in a lodging house, while Hillmon planned how he might improve his fortune and give Sallie the good things she no doubt deserved. Baldwin let it be known that he would help his old friend and new cousin acquire a stock ranch in the Southwest, if Hillmon could find one. Unfortunately, the Southwest was still prey to Indians, wild animals, and other dangers that a loving bridegroom might want to avoid.

Baldwin advised that before Hillmon set out to seek a suitable ranch he insure his life against these dangers. If this would not save Hillmon's scalp it would at least protect his wife. Baldwin introduced Hillmon to the proper insurance agents, and Hillmon applied for and received policies for $10,000 each from the New York Life Insurance Company and from the Mutual Life Insurance Company of New York. Then, in December, 1878, he left for the Southwest in the sole company of a coadventurer, John H. Brown of Wyandotte, Kansas. They took the Atchison, Topeka & Santa Fe to Wichita,

where they hired a wagon and horses. Hillmon returned to Lawrence for a few days in January and in February. While there, he again saw the insurance agents and obtained a third policy—this one for $5,000—from the Connecticut Mutual Life Insurance Company. On the urging of one of the agents, and after some protest, Hillmon allowed himself to be vaccinated against smallpox on February 20. This kept him in Lawrence for a few more days; but about the first of March he went back to Wichita, where he again met Brown, and the two of them headed into the south-Kansas country.

On March 17—St. Patrick's Day—1879, at a campfire on Crooked Creek near Medicine Lodge, Hillmon was accidentally shot and killed. Or so it was claimed. The three insurance companies, which owed his widow $25,000 if it were so, were doubtful that the dead man at the campfire was Hillmon. They knew of two or three Kansans who had recently tried to fake death for the insurance money that was in it.

In 1879 Medicine Lodge had not yet become famous as the home of Carry Nation, "The Smasher," or of "Sockless" Jerry Simpson, the Populist leader; but the editor of its new weekly paper, being of a literary and sardonic turn of mind, had made a somewhat lasting commentary on the time and the place by naming his paper the Medicine Lodge *Cresset,* after the cressets of oil which, according to Milton, were used to light the palaces of hell. The cynicism of that christening was shared by the insurance companies whenever they received an unusual claim from Kansas country.

Sallie Hillmon and Cousin Levi Baldwin insisted that the body *was* Hillmon's. There was only one actual witness to the truth—Brown—and he told two contradictory stories. After about a year of fruitless negotiation, Sallie Hillmon filed suit for her money. In the next twenty-three years the case was tried six times, before six different juries, and went twice to the United States Supreme Court. For three quarters of a century it has been a "leading case" in the law of evidence.

What aroused the suspicions of the insurance companies from the first was the fact that Baldwin and

Hillmon had themselves sought out agents and asked for the policies, whereas all good prospects were expected to wait for agents to seek them out. Later investigations revealed that Levi Baldwin, the reputed cattleman with money, was in fact bankrupt, or at least very hard-pressed by his creditors. One of them he had told—in March, 1879, before Hillmon's death was reported—that he and Hillmon "had a scheme under 'brogue' and that if it worked out all right he was all right." After Hillmon's death was reported, Baldwin put off another creditor by saying that he had arranged to get $10,000 of Hillmon's life insurance. Worst of all (or, from their point of view, best), the insurance investigators learned that in the summer or fall of 1878, before Hillmon applied for his insurance, Baldwin had allegedly had an odd conversation with a doctor. He wanted to know how long it would take a dead body to decompose after it was buried; and then he had archly asked if it would not be "a good scheme to get insured for all you can, and get someone to represent you as dead, and then skip out for Africa or some other damn place?" All that might have been in jest, but subsequent events aroused a natural suspicion that it was in earnest.

We can be certain of very few of the facts in the case, but it is at least safe to say that Hillmon and Brown had no adequate conception of the litigation they were starting when they left Lawrence in December, 1878. Hillmon might have had some foreknowledge of his coming fame, because for the first time in his life he began a diary. (Cynical people believed he wrote the diary just for the purpose of having it planted on "his" dead body, where of course it was found.) It wasn't a very great diary. Despite the fact that he and Brown were going, so they said, to look for a stock ranch, there was not much in the diary about that. The entries chiefly described the weather and the country.

January 6... This kind of weather will make one almost curse camp life, and himself for being so silly as to start on a trip of this kind during the winter months. . . . The sun goes down tonight dark with snow and wind. I think it has been as blustery an afternoon as I have ever witnessed. This kind of weather is what will condemn this part of the country for stock. It will be almost impossible to save near all of the stock . . . .

February 8 . . . I think I have never did as hard work in my life as I have done in the past six weeks. It is killing me almost by inches to loaf around and do nothing as I have been doing of late. . . .

February 23 [back home in Lawrence] . . . Don't see as there is any good to grow out of me trying to keep track of my misdeeds, while I am apt to err as any one. And that I would be sure ashamed not to make a memorandum of, and only show up the best parts as others have done before me. . . .

That was the last entry in the diary when it was found in the dead man's clothing at Crooked Creek. Hillmon and Brown had made camp there on the evening of March 16. The nearest farmer, about three quarters of a mile away, called on them the next morning. In the afternoon, according to Brown, the two spent some time shooting. About sundown, Brown said later, he went to put the gun in the wagon and somehow caught the hammer of the gun and discharged it. Hillmon, standing by the campfire some twelve feet away, was hit in the back of the head and killed. Brown seized him by the arms and swung him away from the fire, but could not save his life or prevent his face from being singed by the flames. Brown's actions then were all very prompt and correct. He immediately went for the farmer who had called on them, and next morning Brown and the farmer went for a justice of the peace, George Washington Paddock. An inquest was held on the spot. Then they took the body to Medicine Lodge, the nearest burying ground, where another inquest was held. Brown wrote the widow a proper letter and gave it to Paddock to send to her:

Medicine Lodge, March 19, 1879

Mrs. S. E. Hillmon:

I am sorry to state the news that I have to state to you. John was shot and killed accidentally by a gun as I went to take it out [*sic*] of the wagon, about 15 miles north of this place. I had him dressed in his best clothes, and buried in Medicine Lodge graveyard. I shall wait here until Mr. Paddock hears from you. If you will leave me to take charge of the team, I will dispose of them to the best advantage, and take the proceeds, and when I come back to Lawrence I will relate the sad news to you. Probably you have heard of it before you get this letter.

Yours truly,
JOHN H. BROWN

Levi Baldwin came to Medicine Lodge at once, without Sallie, and he and Brown neatly fenced the grave. Then three men came from Lawrence to view the corpse for the insurance companies. They insisted that the body be disinterred, and that being done, they promptly declared that it was not Hillmon. Because of this dispute the body was sent to an undertaker in Lawrence, where it was finally seen by the "widow," minutely examined by physicians, and elaborately photographed.

A third and much more formal inquest was held. Brown, Baldwin, Sallie, and about a dozen others identified the body as Hillmon's. Honest persons at Medicine Lodge and elsewhere who had seen Brown and Hillmon on their trip said the body was Hillmon's, or at least that of the man they had seen with Brown. But the insurance companies produced two or three dozen persons who had known Hillmon at Lawrence or other places, who said the body was not his. The undisputed facts were that the corpse was wearing Hillmon's clothes except for his hat, which had been burned, and his shoes, which were somehow lost. The corpse measured five feet eleven inches; the face was marred by burns, but a perfect set of teeth was preserved, and there was a vaccination scab on the arm. The measurement corresponded with Hillmon's height as stated on the insurance policies, but an insurance doctor and some other witnesses swore that Hillmon was actually only five feet nine. (The insurance doctor said he had forgotten to report the shorter measurement to the company until the dispute arose.) There was medical testimony to the effect that Hillmon's vaccination in Lawrence in February would not have left a scab like the one on the body; but the effect of this was undoubtedly lost on the jury because one of the insurance doctors had carefully removed the scab from the body and never returned it. There was a nose scar that some said they remembered on Hillmon; but there was no sign of other scars and marks that Hillmon was said to have had. In particular there was much testimony that Hillmon had been missing a tooth. Sallie denied that; she said her husband's teeth were perfect, like those in the dead body. Sallie was not very good at descriptions. Before the body had arrived at Lawrence the insurance men had tried to get her to describe her husband, but she would say only that he had more hair than her questioner, who was bald. The insurance witnesses, on the other hand, were precise in their recollections of Hillmon's physical peculiarities—considerably more precise, indeed, than they were when cross-examined about the equally obvious peculiarities of other locally well-known persons.

With some of this evidence before them and the insurance lawyers in back of them, the inquest jury brought in a finding that the body was that of an unknown man *feloniously* shot by John H. Brown. The effect of this verdict on Brown was impressive. He went for help to his father, who lived in Wyandotte, and wrote another letter to the "widow":

Mirs Hillmon i would like to now where Johny is and How that business is and what i shall doe if any thing. Let me now threw my Father.

JOHN H. BROWN

His father sent him to a locally influential lawyer-politician named Buchan—the Honorable State Senator W. J. Buchan. In the many trials of the case the insurance lawyers liked to refer to Buchan as Brown's "own attorney"; but what pay Buchan received—some $600 or $700—came from the insurance companies. The court of appeals called his conduct "unprofessional," but he seems to have thought of himself as an

CONTINUED ON PAGE 73

A letter from Medicine Lodge told Sallie Hillmon that John H. Brown (far left, with Hillmon) had killed her husband.

The last old soldiers of the Revolution were fast fading away when Benson J. Lossing set out to catch history alive—in 1,100 pictures and 700,000 words

Historian on the Double

By JOHN T. CUNNINGHAM

With a foreword by ALLAN NEVINS

Nobody would list Benson J. Lossing among the important American historians. But he has an unassailable place among the most useful servants of our historical studies. When he set out on the laborious travels that resulted in the publication of the two large volumes of the *Pictorial Field-Book of the American Revolution,* he had two motives, one patriotic and the other historical. He had noted with regret how little Americans knew about the struggles and sacrifices that had given them place as an independent nation. Citizens of Boston knew nothing of Kings Mountain in South Carolina, where the Tory forces met defeat; citizens of North Carolina and Georgia knew little about the battlefields of Massachusetts and New York. Lossing roamed for more than 8,000 miles through the thirteen original states, traversing rough mountains, deep pine forests, plantation country, and prairies, seeking out every patriot shrine, evading no labor, spending without stint from his slender savings. He made a record of unmatchable scope and variety. He made the

For the frontispiece of his Pictorial Field-Book of the Revolution, *Lossing made a decorative plate of typical uniforms (opposite). In the center is, naturally, an American; the four flanking figures are identified in the margins. Below are an Indian and a militiaman. Right: Lossing as a Vassar College trustee, c. 1870.*

most veracious sketch we possess of Fort Herkimer, at Herkimer, New York, and of the mansion of Governor John Hancock on Beacon Hill in Boston. He talked with veterans everywhere, gathering many a personal reminiscence of value. His volumes, with 1,100 wood engravings of his own drawings of scenes, personages, and relics of the Revolution, admirably supplemented his careful narrative. Without extreme hyperbole, the editor of this magazine remarked recently: "He was a one-man AMERICAN HERITAGE." Lossing lived to issue a useful *Field-Book of the War of 1812* and three volumes on the history of the Civil War. He was one of the first men to grasp the benefits of marrying fresh and authentic historical illustrations to a scholarly text.

It is with good reason that the Huntington Library and other great repositories have collected and preserved them for research. The Huntington has by far the largest body of Lossing materials. Among them are 1,000 of his original drawings and water colors on which the engravings in his books were based; some of the best of these are reproduced—for the first time, so far as is known—with this article. In sum, the Lossing papers constitute an enduring memorial to one of the most laborious and self-sacrificing writers upon our past. But his career is too little known today—an oversight that this essay should do much to remedy. —*Allan Nevins*

Fort Ticonderoga, on Lake Champlain, excited all of Lossing's impulses as patriot, historian, and artist. There he interviewed an aged survivor of the Revolution, Isaac Rice, who kept body and soul together by acting as a guide in the ruined fortress. "Mr. Rice sat down in the cool shadow . . . while I sketched his person and scenery in the distance," Lossing wrote. He also provided his readers with a ground plan of Ticonderoga as it was in 1775 when Ethan Allen captured it (below, left), and sketched "the present features" of the ruins (below).

IN JUNE, 1848, Benson J. Lossing of Poughkeepsie, New York, stopped his horse near Greenwich, Connecticut, to look at curious bramble-entwined steps cut into a hillside at a place known locally as Horse Neck. Nearby, a white-haired man leaned on a garden gate. Lossing asked him about the steps. "Short cut to the church up there," the old man replied, pointing to a steeple atop the hill. And then, abruptly, he began to relate a famous incident of the American Revolution, when General Israel Putnam had ridden madly down that hill to escape the British.

Advancing redcoats had surprised Putnam on the morning of March 26, 1779, while he was shaving in the nearby home of Ebenezer Mead of the local militia. Putnam dropped his razor, and with lather foaming on his cheeks, dashed outside to rally a defense. His soldiers held briefly near the church before fleeing, every man for himself. Putnam desperately spurred his horse down the steep slope, past the steps where a militiaman crouched.

"I heard Old Put cursing the British between his teeth!" the old man exclaimed.

"Tell me, please, who I am talking to," Lossing asked with growing excitement.

"They call me General Mead," the old man replied. A shiver went through Lossing: General Ebenezer Mead of the Connecticut militia, Putnam's host and admirer, alive and on the spot where he had seen history pass!

56

A few miles south of the southern tip of Lake Champlain, Lossing sketched the site of old Fort Ann—by his time a prosperous farmstead and nearly empty of military vestiges. On the basis of his rough sketch, the historian made a finished, colored drawing (above); from that a woodcut for his book was engraved (below). Note the ghostly wagon, which takes more material shape in the engraving.

As he drove rapidly home to Poughkeepsie, Lossing reasoned that if there was a clearheaded General Mead still alive in Horse Neck, Connecticut, there had to be his counterparts elsewhere—in Saratoga, in Boston, in the Carolinas and Virginia. He would find them, sketch them, write their tales!

Lossing already had modest writing and illustrating credits. In Poughkeepsie he had been active as a journalist, and his pedantic *Outline History of the*

Fine Arts, published in 1840, plus a series of thin illustrated paperbacks, *Seventeen Hundred and Seventy-Six,* had earned some literary attention. His major talent was as an artist, and he was well known in New York as the senior partner of the firm of Lossing and Barritt, one of the city's pioneer wood-engraving companies when it was founded in 1843.

He took pride in his knowledge of history, all of it learned in spare hours between his daily work as a wood engraver and his nighttime writing efforts. But in contrast to his own intense interest, he felt that most readers found history dull.

The chance meeting with General Mead kept Lossing awake that night, drawing rough sketches and laying out a different kind of history book. He planned a series of trips to the principal areas of the Revolution, seeking the "animate and inanimate relics of

Hubbardton Battlefield, near Rutland, Vermont, where a tough battle was lost by the patriots in July, 1777, looked peaceful enough when Lossing got there.

the war, both of which were fading away." Interspersed with a narrative describing Revolutionary War events, he would mix eyewitness tales of survivors and an account of his own travels. Lossing hoped that "a record of the pilgrimage, interwoven with that of the facts of past history" would appeal to many "who could not be otherwise decoyed into the apparently arid and flowerless domains of mere history."

The very next day he took the idea and the sketches to Harper and Brothers in New York. Harper's agreed to underwrite his expenses and to publish his book. Thus, within twenty-four hours, if Lossing did not romanticize in his later memory, his notable *Pictorial Field-Book of the Revolution* was conceived.

Leaving his partner in charge of their engraving business, Lossing left New York for Albany on July 24, 1848, for his first field trip—to Saratoga and Ticon-

deroga, into Canada as far as Quebec, and thence southwestward into upper New York state. With him went "a young lady, my traveling companion"—very probably his wife, Alice, since there is no evidence that he was given to philandering. At any rate, he allowed little time for romance. He set a gruelling pace, early to bed and early to rise, with no time for casual sight-seeing or rest. He believed in concentrated effort, and at the age of thirty-five he had the stamina to make fourteen- to sixteen-hour workdays possible.

Aboard the steamboat to Albany with Lossing was a "remnant of a regiment of Volunteers returning home, weary and spirit-broken, from the battlefields of Mexico." Busy Albany welcomed the heroes with booming cannon and blaring bands, but Lossing was eager to get on with another, older war.

At the Waterford ferry, north of Albany, "a funny

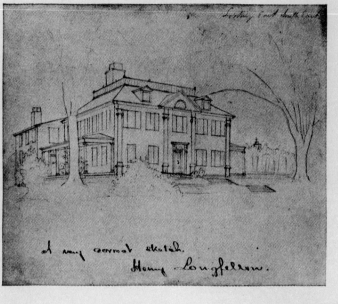

little water-man, full of wine and wit, or something stronger and coarser, offered to row us across in his rickety skiff. I demanded the price for ferriage. 'Five thousand dollars,' hiccoughed the Charon. I did not object to the price, but, valuing safety at a higher figure, sought the owner of a pretty craft nearby." Lossing gave the ferryman a "brief temperance lecture," and in return was consigned "to the safekeeping of him whom the old painters limned with a hoof and a horn, a beak and a scorpion tail."

Near Saratoga, the historian met his first eyewitness of that famous Revolutionary War encounter. She was "Mrs. J——n," ninety-two years old, with "soft blue eye" and a "memory remarkably tenacious." When General John Burgoyne's army rampaged down their valley in October, 1777, Mrs. J——n and her parents hid in a nearby swamp, fearful that Indians or Tories

might murder them. Her young fiancé was off with the Americans preparing to intercept Burgoyne.

When the family returned home, Mrs. J——n told Lossing, all was desolation. "Our crops and our cattle, our sheep, hogs, and horses, were all gone . . . yet we . . . thanked God sincerely that our house and barns were not destroyed." She eventually married her young soldier, but now had long been

N. Eastern view of West Bridge New Haven

widowed and living on a pension. With quivering lip, she told her visitor that "the government has been very kind to me in my poverty and old age."

A few days later, Lossing encountered Isaac Rice, a ragged veteran who had no cause for joy over his treatment by his country. Rice appeared unexpectedly amid the rubble of Fort Ticonderoga, just as Lossing was about to hire a professional guide to take him through "the gray old ruins." The aged soldier said that as a lad he had done garrison duty in Ticonderoga under Major General Arthur St. Clair and "was in the field at Saratoga" in June, 1777. Now he was eighty-five years old, with his pension cut off by bureaucratic red tape. Lossing sketched the old man braced against a crum-

bling wall. Later the artist returned to sketch the fort at sunset. A soft footstep startled him; it was Rice, back to sit in the fort as he always did on pleasant nights. The old soldier showed Lossing a room in the ruins where he hoped to clear away the rubbish so that next year he could sell cakes, beer, and fruit to visitors. He spoke "with a low voice, as if afraid some rival might hear his business plans." All he needed, Rice said, was eight dollars.

Saratoga and Ticonderoga solidified the pattern for the entire *Field-Book*. Lossing conscientiously tramped across the battlefield and through the fort, measuring distances and calculating the effect of terrain on troop movements. Few historians have related geography

60

Opposite, above: Lossing, not to be stayed from his appointed rounds by either snow or rain, sometimes sketched on a folding table under an umbrella. His choice of subjects—Revolutionary or otherwise—often proved Lossing's sharp sense of the dramatic: Robinson House, on the Hudson (seen opposite in both water color and engraving), which was Benedict Arnold's headquarters at the time of his defection; the Old Tower in Newport, Rhode Island (above), built in early colonial times for mysterious purposes (and still there today); and Frances Slocum (right), who was kidnapped by Delaware Indians in 1778 and found by her family in 1837 after she had "led a roving life, and loved it."

to history better than he. Although he was only an amateur cartographer, his meticulous maps were a major contribution to the historical annals of the day.

Lossing sketched constantly, paying close attention to details of architecture and location of buildings. He jotted marginal notes on shadings, foliage, and other factors that would help him make woodcuts for the book. His drawings were handsome, accurate renderings of just what he saw—rain pelting down on a scene; even a bull that chased him from the battlefield at Bennington.

Lossing went overland through lower Canada to sketch the fort at Chambly, where General Richard Montgomery had subdued the British garrison in October, 1775, before the subsequent successful siege of St. Johns. Someone directed Lossing to a remarkable man named François Yest, who lived nearby.

Yest, born in Quebec in 1752, claimed to have witnessed two wars: he had, he said, seen both Wolfe's storming of Quebec in 1759 and Montgomery's capture of Fort Chambly in 1775. He had farmed the same ground near Chambly since 1777. Lossing sketched him. "When I presented him with a silver coin, he laughed like a pleased child"; but when someone offered Yest a glass of brandy, the old man became angry. He had signed a temperance pledge a year before and planned to keep it the rest of his life, after ninety-five years of nonabstinence. "For that," wrote Lossing, "I pressed the hard hand of François Yest with a firmer grasp when I bade him adieu."

Lossing visited Quebec to sketch scenes of the desperate and unsuccessful siege of the city by Montgomery and Benedict Arnold in the late months of 1775. He then headed west on the St. Lawrence River

Fascinated by the setting of Horatio Gates's great victory over Burgoyne at Saratoga, Lossing meticulously rendered Freeman's Farm (above), where much of the fighting occurred; the grave of the gallant British General Simon Fraser (left); and General Gates's headquarters (below).

to Niagara Falls. Niagara had few Revolutionary associations, but Lossing sketched the Suspension Bridge, still unfinished in 1848, and rode the bobbing little tourist craft *Maid of the Mist* in the turbulence directly below the falls. A week before, a young couple had been married on the boat. "What an altar before which to make nuptial vows!" Lossing noted.

Near Canajoharie in New York's Mohawk Valley, Lossing met seventy-nine-year-old Jacob Dievendorff, who had been eleven years old when nearly five hundred Indians and a few Tories sacked his village on July 9, 1781. An Indian felled Jacob with a tomahawk, sliced the scalp off the back of his head, and taking the grisly trophy, left the boy for dead.

Dievendorff had survived to become a wealthy landholder. He sat on a half-bushel basket in his barn while Lossing sketched him from the front to show what appeared to be a full head of hair. Dievendorff then turned to reveal horrible scars where the scalp had been cut sixty-eight years before. The visitor sketched that view, too.

Lossing was back in New York City by September 1. Already he had hundreds of sketches and enough data to fill three hundred book pages with maps, illustrations, travel stories, historical narrative, and a blend of folklore and curious factual detail. His work was by no means merely a matter of finding survivors; at every stop he had consulted or borrowed materials,

Prolific but selective, Lossing copied —but did not use in his text—the portrait below of a British officer. On a southern trip, he found nothing but ruins of the once magnificent Tryon Palace in New Bern, North Carolina; but he based an accurate sketch on the original plans, borrowed from the architect's grandson. Kings Mountain, in South Carolina, he drew as he saw it in 1849.

King's Mountain Battle ground

Captain Asgill.

particularly letters, original documents, and diaries.

A brief September interlude took Lossing to Morristown and Springfield in New Jersey, then as far as Wyoming Valley in Pennsylvania. At Morristown, he passed an evening with lively, eighty-three-year-old Gabriel Ford, son of the widow who had owned the mansion where Washington and his staff passed the dreadfully cold winter of 1779–80. Mrs. Ford and her four young children had retained two rooms for themselves. Gabriel was fourteen at the time.

Ford entertained Lossing "until a late hour." He told of Washington's constant solicitude for Mrs. Ford and her family; if alarms sounded in Morristown, "he always went to her room, drew the curtains close, and soothed her by assurances of safety." When the General left the mansion in the spring, he asked Mrs. Ford whether everything had been returned to her. "All but

one silver table-spoon," she replied. Soon after, a messenger brought a silver spoon with the initials *G. W.*

Washington told young Ford the countersign each evening, so that he could play in the village after the guards were posted. One night as he returned at about nine o'clock, the boy saw Colonel Alexander Hamilton stopped by the guard. The Colonel had been visiting Miss Betsy Schuyler, who spent that winter in Morristown and later became Mrs. Hamilton. "Thoughts of her undoubtedly expelled the countersign from his head," said Ford. The guard knew Hamilton well, but refused to admit him without the proper word. The Colonel stood in embarrassment, then spotted young Gabriel and said in a whisper: "Master Ford, is that you? . . . Give me the countersign." The boy complied and Hamilton passed it on to the guard, who reluctantly let the Colonel pass.

After Morristown, Lossing stopped at Springfield, site of spirited military action in June, 1780. The oldest inhabitant was Gilbert Edwards, a "half grown boy" when American troops fought the British there on June 23. Edwards did not purport to be a hero. Rather, he had shown good Yankee shrewdness: he sold apples to the militiamen headed east to fight the invaders.

Lossing set out late in September for New England, "the nursery of the Revolutionary spirit." He stopped in Danbury, Connecticut, and there found a genuine eyewitness jackpot: three men who had been in the village on April 26, 1777, when British troops put the torch to every house except those occupied by Tories. Levi Osborn, eighty-six, and Ezra Foote, eighty-four, both victims of the 1777 holocaust, offered little more than conversation. Far more interesting was the old Tory Joseph Dibble, who was approaching his hundredth birthday when Lossing called.

Loyal to King George, Dibble had joyously welcomed the invaders, who naturally spared his house and barn. Lossing sketched Dibble, perhaps unconsciously giving him a sly "Tory" look that is preserved in the book. The old man admitted that he had been "greatly despised" by his neighbors, and told of being taken to a river and ducked until dawn. He was a bachelor—and told Lossing that he "intended to remain one all the days of his life."

Boston, "classic ground of the Revolution," provided rich material for Lossing's narrative, but he found no survivors there. He learned, however, that David Kinnison, a participant in the Tea Party of December, 1773, was alive in Chicago at the astonishing age of 111 years, nine months. Lossing corresponded with Kinnison and received his picture and signature, plus a long record of Revolutionary War activity at Bunker Hill, Long Island, Germantown, and elsewhere. Kinnison had been married four times, had fathered twenty-two children, and had learned to read at the age of sixty. One of Kinnison's friends reported that the flame of liberty still burned in the old man. He had just urged a Chicago abolition meeting to seek freedom for "the black boys."

Lexington, Massachusetts, boasted two cousins who had seen the fighting on the green on the nineteenth of April, 1775. Jonathan Harrington, seventeen years old at the time, played the fife that summoned the volunteers. That was his first and last deed in the war. His cousin Abijah Harrington, too young to fight, was ordered by his mother "to go near enough, and be safe," to bring back information on two older brothers in the battle. He watched the battle with boyish delight and reported to his mother that both brothers survived.

Visiting Cambridge to sketch Washington's headquarters, Lossing met Henry Wadsworth Longfellow, who, not incidentally, lived in the house. Longfellow came out to express "warm approval" of the visitor's task. (Later the poet sent a tart note of correction on a proof of the drawing and the accompanying text, noting that Lossing had left out a chimney and had erroneously called him a "professor of Oriental languages" at Harvard, whereas he actually taught modern European languages. Lossing made both corrections before publication.)

Although he had accomplished much, Lossing realized that his greatest task still lay ahead. He had to tour the battlefields of the South, with winter coming on and with travel conditions that were uncertain even in the best of seasons. Except for Williamsburg, Richmond, and Yorktown, little had been published for national audiences about the war in that portion of the country: Lossing must be credited with writing the first major account of the Revolution in the South.

He bought a horse named Charley, hitched him to a light dearborn wagon, and drove him aboard a South Amboy ferry on November 22, 1848. They plodded across New Jersey, through Princeton and Trenton, and on to Philadelphia. There Lossing rose early and made an eagerly anticipated visit to Carpenters' Hall. He was stunned by a sign on the door that read "C. J. WOLPERT & CO., AUCTIONEERS." He wrote indignantly: "What a desecration! Covering the facade of the very Temple of Freedom with the placards of groveling mammon!"

Independence Hall, however, satisfied the patriot in Lossing. He climbed the steeple and leaned against the cracked Liberty Bell while he thought about the Declaration of Independence. He came down to earth and walked Philadelphia's streets, sorry that so few people seemed to remember anything about the city's days of glory.

The historian rode on. Between Annapolis and Washington he followed a curious public highway. In the first thirteen miles he opened fifteen gates, placed across the road not for tolls but to foil wandering cattle. A boy by the roadside advised him that gates were "pretty tick" ahead—and they were. The annoyed traveller encountered, in all, fifty-three gates in the thirty-six miles between the two cities.

In Washington, Lossing had the privilege of an hour with President James Polk; it was a visit prompted not by "the foolish desire to see the exalted," but rather by the hope that the President would give him a letter of introduction to people in his native North Carolina. Polk complied.

A stop in Charles City, Virginia, near Richmond, turned up a treasure. Lossing spent the evening in the

CONTINUED ON PAGE 78

INCIDENT
on the ISTHMUS

Back when Panama was a jumping-off
place for Eldorado, a piece of
melon became a symbol that led to a massacre.
Its seeds of anti-Yankee resentment
are still bearing fruit

By JOHN CASTILLO KENNEDY

ILLUSTRATED FOR AMERICAN HERITAGE BY LEONARD SLONEVSKY

In the telegraph room of the Panama Railroad station the operator was tapping out an anguished message to the company's chief engineer in Aspinwall, miles away across the Isthmus: bullets were coming through the room, it said, and the telegrapher added, "I shall be shot. I must go." But there was no place to go. It was no longer possible even to send a telegram; outside, a mob had just torn down the telegraph wires.

Downstairs, in the darkness, the battering of the doors continued. Men were piled in a human barricade against them, while scores of others crouched on the floor, trying to escape the bullets coming up from outside. At the back of the building a group of natives was bringing burning coals to set the building on fire.

White men, women, and children at the mercy of a mob of natives—either a scene from poor-grade fiction or, if true in fact, surely the by-product of long years of oppression. The scene was true enough in this case, but it came in 1856, early in the relationship between the United States and Panama (then a state of New Granada, which later became Colombia). The relationship had begun in the late 1840's, when thousands of Americans first began hurrying across the Isthmus en route to the gold fields of California.

Earlier on this Tuesday, April 15, 1856, nine hundred and forty people, more than half of them women and children, had arrived at the port of Aspinwall (present-day Colon), the United States Mail Steamship Company's Atlantic terminus. They had gone directly to the waiting coaches of the American-owned Panama Railroad, and four hours later—at about four-thirty—they were at the railroad's depot on the Pacific.

They could go no farther for the time being. The Pacific Mail Steamship Company's *John L. Stephens*, which would take them to San Francisco, was anchored in the bay, but the steamer *Taboga*, which would ferry them out to the *Stephens*, was stranded in the mud at the foot of the railroad wharf and would remain mired until the tide came in late that night.

The railroad terminal was situated along the beach three eighths of a mile north of the walled city of Panama. The station building was a split-level structure built of plain pine boards. The lower floor, seven feet off the ground, was primarily a freight room, with a baggage room and a railroad and ticket office at the eastern, or beach, end of the building. On that same end, stairs led up to three more offices and a telegraph room on the second floor.

It had not been built with passenger comfort in mind. Nowhere in the building, or anywhere else on the grounds, was there anything resembling a waiting room, unless one cared to sit on a trunk in the baggage room. The ticket office opened onto a four-foot-wide platform on the north side of the building; on steamer days the Pacific Mail line took over the office to process the tickets of its passengers as they filed past outside. Passengers could then board the ferry or wait on shore. Few of them went into the city of Panama; that derelict town of eight thousand or so people, ninety per cent of them Negro or Indian, was avoided by all but the most curious.

It had not always been that way. In the early days of the Gold Rush, before the railroad was finished and before the Pacific Mail had enough ships to accommodate the traffic, Panama had been transformed into an American city, with two and three thousand Americans at a time waiting—sometimes for weeks on end —for transportation to San Francisco. Panama City's Calle de la Merced was lined with American hotels, saloons, and gambling "hells," and filled with swaggering, insolent gringos. By the mid-fifties, however, the American-run establishments had disappeared from the city; nowadays, passengers usually went no farther than those hotels and saloons, owned by Americans and other white foreigners, which had sprung up along the beach between the fenced compound of the railroad station and the walled city. These establishments faced "Main Street," which led to a gate on the south side of the compound.

On this particular Tuesday afternoon in 1856, one of the steerage passengers with time on his hands was an ill-tempered, hard-drinking man named Jack Oliver. He and a group of rowdy companions went

"José Luna stood his ground. 'Pay me my money,' he said, 'and let us be square.'"

first to the Golden Eagle saloon, about two hundred yards down Main Street from the railroad station. They left the Golden Eagle, fairly drunk, at about five-thirty. Some native vendors were gathered outside. As he wandered past, Oliver picked up a slice of watermelon from the tray of one José Luna; he ate part of it and walked on.

Luna followed him, demanding payment—a dime. (American dimes were the most common currency on the Isthmus.) Oliver ignored him. When the native persisted, Oliver pushed him away and told him, "Don't bother me. Kiss my arse."

José Luna, a strapping, twenty-nine-year-old mulatto, stood his ground. "Take care; we are not here in the United States," he warned Oliver. "Pay me my money and let us be square."

Oliver drew his pistol and snarled, "I'll pay you with a shot."

Luna had a dagger out just as quickly. Friends from both sides tried to intervene. One of the Americans offered to pay the dime but was ignored. Then one of Luna's friends, a "light-colored" man named Miguel Habrahan, stepped in and grabbed Oliver's pistol. It went off in the scuffle that followed, but no one was hit. Frightened, Habrahan broke away and, still clutching the pistol, ran up the beach toward the boat-shed in front of the railroad station. The Americans ran after him, Oliver in the lead, his companions shouting, "Kill him! Kill him!" But as always when there was trouble between Americans and natives, Luna and the other blacks faded away.

For such altercations were not unprecedented; over the years there had been a number of incidents involving gunplay. Nor was there now, at six o'clock, anything else to mark the day as unusual. In the ticket office, clerks were busy stamping passengers' tickets; about six hundred had filed past the windows, and most of them had boarded the *Taboga* to wait. But there were still more than three hundred—about seventy of them women and children—to be taken care of. Outside, the station grounds were crowded with people who had arrived from San Francisco on the *Cortes* and were waiting for the train to leave for Aspinwall, and with others who had come out from Panama City for the sailing.

On the railroad pier near the station, Captain Allan McLane, the Pacific Mail agent, was chatting with Alexander Center, the railroad superintendent, and William Nelson, another railroad employee. McLane was supervising forty Negroes who were unloading freight and baggage from the train to go aboard the *Stephens*. The scene was busy, crowded, and cheerful.

Meanwhile Oliver went to Ocean House, another saloon, where he had another whiskey and boasted loudly about the watermelon incident. Then, at his companions' urging, he went back with them to the ticket office to have his steamer ticket validated. Miguel Habrahan, having gotten away from him, had doubled back along the beach toward town; what Habrahan did next is still unknown, but suddenly the bells of the Church of Santa Anna, a quarter-mile away in the parish outside the walls of the city, began to peal. Then the alarm bell in the cupola over Gorgona Gate in the city wall began to ring. Within minutes—almost as if by prearranged signal—crowds gathered at the edge of the city, and soon they were rushing toward the railroad station, shouting and waving their arms. They passed through the Cienega, a crowded slum of cane shanties that lay between Santa Anna parish and the station, stretching beachward as far as the saloons and hotels. In the Cienega they found arms and ammunition, and a great many more natives eager to join them.

The mob had learned somehow that Oliver had gone to Ocean House, so they headed there first. There were still a few Americans in the bar. (But not Oliver; his ticket validated, he had boarded the *Taboga* and had fallen asleep.) There were also some American families resting in the hotel rooms upstairs. The mob was headed for the barroom; some of the blacks were already firing into it. Inside, James Quinn, the Dublin-born bartender, and one or two armed Americans began to fire back.

All the more excited by the return fire, the natives —machetes and knives flashing, guns firing—forced their way into Ocean House, grappling with the men inside and smashing the rude furniture of the barroom. Most of the combatants, black and white, were ignorant of the fighting's immediate cause, but even if Oliver had still been there, his capture by the mob would not have slaked their anger. All the hatred and resentment against arrogant Americans who lit their cigars at candles in the cathedral, rudely disrupted religious processions, challenged local authorities and scorned local taxes, shoved natives out of the way in the streets, cursed and browbeat them, short-changed and refused to pay them—all this had coalesced into an easily fired determination to destroy. The Americans in the Ocean House bar, no longer masters, turned and ran out the back door, then up the beach to the railroad pier and the safety of the *Taboga*.

Having drunk most of the whiskey and made a shambles of everything else at Ocean House, the mob grew and spread. They looted nearby McAllister's store, filling empty bottles from whiskey casks, and surged across the street to pillage another small store called the Triangle. Next were Pacific House and the Golden Eagle saloon, which they attacked with guns,

"A drunken American began to fire his pistol into the air."

stones, and bottles. Upstairs at Pacific House, two men jumped out a back window and ran to safety; the rest of the occupants, mostly women and children, cowered helplessly—but were still safer than a woman they could see running, screaming, in the street below, pursued by a Negro with a bar stool in his hand.

The closest the mob had come to the railroad station was Ocean House, about two hundred feet away; it appeared that the destruction would be confined to the commercial buildings facing the Cienega. There had been no indication that the station would be attacked, and there was good reason to suppose that it would not be, for the natives held the Panama Railroad in considerable awe: it possessed more power and authority than the local government, and, until fairly recently, it had done its own ruthless policing of the transit zone. The station, within the fenced compound, sheltered hundreds of people, who, the natives might reasonably suppose, would resist any attack.

This was hard for those in the compound to realize, however, and as it grew dark and the rioting continued outside, they began to panic. A drunken American at the head of the station steps began to fire his pistol into the air. Inside, those few who were armed had their pistols out and ready; others were demanding arms and ammunition from the railroad and steamship officials. Captain McLane tried to quiet them, urging those with pistols not to fire them for fear of inviting retaliation, insisting that the station would not be attacked. He told them that he had sent a messenger to Colonel Garrido, the chief of police, and that it was only a matter of time until he and his men would arrive and put an end to the riot.

But the minutes went by and the police did not come. A group of about fifteen men, unwilling to wait any longer, went out—unarmed—to try to rescue the women and children in the upper floors of Ocean House and Pacific House. They were met by twice their number of natives and were stoned and driven back; as they tried to re-enter the depot in the darkness, they were fired upon by their jittery fellow Americans. One was shot through the body as he came up the steps, and another through the leg as he went back to get the wounded man.

In the darkness inside the station (the ticket office downstairs and the telegraph room upstairs were the only rooms with lights), Captain McLane and William Nelson considered trying to organize a few men to preserve order and prevent any acts of provocation by the Americans, but by now organization was utterly impossible. Everyone who could possibly get into the station had crowded in—nearly three hundred men and women—and now that it was dark, they were hysterical with the fear that the natives would rush the station. They were as unreasoning as the mob.

Superintendent Center had distributed, reluctantly, all the weapons that could be found in the station: a double-barrelled shotgun, a pair of pistols, a saber, and fourteen old flintlock muskets that were rusty and barely usable. Thus armed, and well fortified with whiskey, some of the men began darting out and firing into the huts of the Cienega, and then rushing back. Inside, many were frantically searching for family or friends from whom they had been separated.

Shortly after seven, the United States consul, Colonel Thomas Ward, rode up on horseback with his secretary, Theodore de Sabla; they had ridden out from town along the beach to avoid the rioting mob in the Cienega. They found twenty or more Americans just outside the gate of the railroad compound. A cannon loaded with boiler rivets (for lack of any other ammunition) had been dragged up in front of the gate, in a position commanding the principal street of the Cienega. Pistols and muskets were much in evidence. Men, talking wildly of killing the "savages," were firing reckless shots at the native huts. Every round fired brought more shots in return from natives in trees bordering the Cienega.

Colonel Ward was a grizzled old man with a wooden leg and a stump for an arm. He was not popular with the American residents of Panama; he was much too blunt and outspoken. He assessed the situation quickly. He considered Center's distribution of arms weak and irresponsible. Angrily, he ordered the Americans to put away their guns, to go back inside, to avoid further provoking the natives in any way. His voice was commanding and his authority evident; they put down their weapons, and the man tending the cannon said he would fire only if directly attacked.

Ward was informed that the governor of Panama, Francisco Fábrega, had come out to the Cienega. He sent de Sabla to fetch him, while he himself rode toward the bands of Negroes drawing up to return the Americans' fire. Impervious to the danger, he gave orders as brusquely as he had to the Americans; the natives grew quiet and began to lay down their arms. Firing had ceased on both sides. For a brief moment, it seemed as if the riot could be controlled.

De Sabla had entered the Cienega and located Governor Fábrega, who was as resentful of American arrogance as any other Panamanian; he did not care to be fetched to the Consul's presence by the Consul's secretary. And he had a still more compelling, though unvoiced, reason for being reluctant to act: he was a white man, a member of one of the few remaining Castilian families in Panama and the state's only white official. The mob's anger was now directed at the white Americans; he was afraid that any move on his part to restrain them would make them turn on the native whites as well. He refused to go.

De Sabla went back to tell Ward, who said that he would meet the Governor halfway, in Main Street. The Consul and his secretary rode into the street together and then de Sabla went on to tell the Governor that Colonel Ward was waiting for him.

This time Fábrega agreed, with persuasion, to go, and they went back through the Cienega toward Main Street. There was more firing in the distance. As they reached the street, just below Pacific House, de Sabla suggested that it would be safer for the Governor to wait while he went on ahead.

It seemed to Colonel Ward that he had been waiting too long for his secretary to come back. Impatient, he decided to go into the Cienega himself to look for the Governor, and so, as de Sabla and the Governor were emerging into the street just beyond Pacific House, Ward, together with William Nelson, was leaving the street and making his way through the cane huts of the Cienega.

In the dark, silent street the Governor waited as de Sabla rode ahead to where they were to meet the Consul. Ahead of him, in the shadows, the secretary saw a band of natives come out into the street. As he stopped for a moment to see what they would do, an American suddenly rushed to the compound gate and fired out at the natives. There was a roar of answering fire from the Cienega, then more fire from the Americans. De Sabla screamed with pain as a musket ball hit his thigh and another glanced off his knee. A third whistled through Governor Fábrega's hat; he turned and ran. In the Cienega, William Nelson threw himself flat on the ground. Colonel Ward was caught in four separate lines of fire, his horse rearing as one ball after another—seven in all—hit it. The horse ran off as Ward, miraculously unharmed, tried his best to hang on with his one arm.

Nelson was a long-time resident of Panama and was well liked by the natives. As he picked himself up he was warned that he had better go home if he hoped to avoid being killed, for the mob was determined now to attack the station itself. He ignored the warning and slipped back into the station. There was now incessant fire from the Cienega on the railroad buildings

69

and yard. As Nelson entered the gate a musket ball struck and broke the arm of a passenger beside him. He went on to tell Ward, who had managed to guide his wounded horse back into the compound, and McLane and the others that the blacks were about to attack the station. Ward had no hope of controlling the riot now; if Colonel Garrido and the police did not come, there was little anyone could do.

In the station the terrified people waited in darkness. They had few weapons, and most of their ammunition had been used up in the irresponsible firing into the Cienega. One plan after another was suggested for escape, but escape was impossible. It was dangerous to stay, but even more dangerous to go outside. And even if they could get to the *Taboga,* there was no assurance that the ferry would not be attacked too.

Shots were coming from every direction, as though the buildings were surrounded. All at once there was a burst of shots from the bushes behind the old blacksmith's shop, a short distance from the station. Then a bugle sounded. Railroad Superintendent Center told those who could hear him that everything was all right: the police had arrived.

But instead of stopping, the firing grew heavier than ever—it was coming in volleys now—as the police bugle sounded again and again. Center ventured outside and, creeping along the side of the building, saw a mob of Negroes coming down the railroad track to attack from the rear. He ran up the steps and into the freight room. It was crowded with terrified people.

He could not even get back out again. The doors were blockaded by terror-stricken Americans. The noise was fantastic—musket balls crashing through the walls, the bugle sounding, the doors suddenly rattling as yelling rioters tried to force them open. Center managed to get from the freight room into the railroad office through a broken panel in the connecting door. As he stepped through, a man fell dead before him; another, hit, clutched his throat and fell.

Smoke filled the station office. Its doors too were blockaded with people. Center turned and went back into the freight room and, climbing up the wall, managed to get on a plank across the ceiling beams. From there he could see outside all too clearly: the police were firing at the building; Colonel Garrido, the Negro police chief, was urging them on.

There was no one left to appeal to but the Governor, and he had gone back into town. (It was later learned that, infuriated at being fired at by the Americans, Fábrega himself had ordered the police to attack the station.) At the mess house, next to the station, Ward, Nelson, and McLane decided to go after the Governor to plead with him to come back and use his

authority to halt the massacre. They set out along the beach, sloshing through the mud flats at the very edge of the water in the hope of avoiding any natives. They had gone a few hundred yards when they were challenged by an armed band of Negroes. As they raised their guns, Nelson quickly told them who he was; the many years of good will and respect he had earned from the natives enabled the three men to pass safely.

At the station, the mob and the police, swarming within the compound, were trying to force their way in through one of the windows of the ticket office. Inside the building, a wounded man named Ewing rested his revolver on the edge of a counter and fired with deliberate aim whenever a head appeared at the window, until all his bullets were gone. There was no holding them off any longer. In possession of the window, they fired down on the passengers lying on the floor. The Americans scrambled wildly to escape, some into the adjoining baggage room and some upstairs, leaving behind ten of their number dead or wounded. The mob poured in through the window and began to strip the bodies of money, keys—everything of value.

At the other end of the building the door to the baggage room had given way too, and in rushed the natives, hacking indiscriminately with machetes. The Americans were completely defenseless, "open to the covetousness and barbarity," as Colonel Ward later put it, "of as rude a people as exist upon the globe." A man was killed trying to get away, and a woman with him was wounded; both were robbed. A minister named Sellwood was shot though the head as he tried to run through the door. Some managed to escape from the building and ran blindly down the beach into the muddy tidelands or back to hide in the trees, only to be found, attacked, and robbed by roving bands of natives.

In the city, Ward, Nelson, and McLane had found the Governor in San Juan de Diós Street, surrounded by a crowd of shouting, vengeful natives. He declined to help, insisting that he could do nothing, that he had no control over the police or the people. Colonel Ward doubtless reminded him that a U.S. ship of war would surely be dispatched to Panama immediately, as a result of the riot. What happened to the city and to the Governor, he intimated, might depend largely on what the Governor did right then.

Fábrega knew well enough what the arrival of the U.S. Navy could mean; he—and a great many other Central Americans—remembered that less than two years before, the U.S. sloop of war *Cyane* had destroyed the town of San Juan del Norte, the Atlantic terminus of the trans-Nicaragua route, in a much smaller dispute between natives and Americans. Reluctantly he agreed to go and do what he could, and he and Mc-

Lane and Nelson set out. Ward stayed in town; he had done all the walking he could do on his wooden leg.

Nothing that had happened before equalled the horror that was going on in the station house now. Once the mob had gained entry there was little more shooting. The main impulse was to rob and loot. The only safety for the stranded passengers lay in pretending to be dead. Doing so, one man felt his clothing being ransacked again and again—ten times, he thought; finally his feet were lifted up and his boots stolen. Any resistance—any movement, even—met with a savage reply. A man seen to move was pounced on. He begged for mercy, but a machete and a club descended on his head simultaneously; a wounded man near him "seemed to hear his skull crash," and the victim rolled over without a groan.

Colonel Garrido, satisfied that he had achieved his objective at the station, had gone to the pier with some of his adjutants and had boarded the *Taboga*. There had been no provocative action from the passengers aboard the stranded ferry steamer; nevertheless, the police chief informed its captain that he had come to disarm the ship. If they gave up their arms the natives would not attack; otherwise he would not be able to control them. The passengers watched helplessly as he collected two pistols, the only ones in evidence, while the ship's cannon was dragged off. A short time later a remarkably similar cannon was set up on shore, loaded, and aimed at the *Taboga*.

It was to this spot that the Governor and the two Americans hurried first, when they finally got back to the station area at about ten o'clock. The Governor ordered the man with the cannon, a huge Negro named Dolores Urriola, to give it up. Urriola refused, insolently telling the Governor that he was going to fire it at the ship. McLane remembered suddenly and thankfully that when the riot first began he had sent two Panamanian women who had come to see the sailing, Señoras Ansoatique and Feraud, aboard the *Taboga* for safety. He quickly whispered to the Governor to tell Urriola that he would be killing his own countrywomen if he fired. That persuaded the Negro to hold his fire, but he would not surrender the cannon.

Nearby some natives were breaking open a black trunk they had dragged from the freight room. Fábrega made no effort to stop them; it was frighteningly evident that, as he had insisted earlier, he no longer had any control over the people. McLane and Nelson went on to the station without him.

Looters were still busy in the freight room and in some of the freight cars. Colonel Garrido and several of the police were drawn up between the station house and the mess house, about to fire a volley at the upper floor. Garrido blustered that they had been fired on and were going to retaliate, but he was disconcerted by the arrival of the two Americans, and he handed them a lantern when Nelson said they would go up and guarantee that there would be no further shooting.

There were four rooms on the second floor. The first, the small telegraph room, was locked and empty; the telegrapher had escaped without harm. A bloody corpse blocked the doorway to the second room. Nelson and McLane managed to shove the door open far enough to step over the body and into the

"They were met by twice their number of natives and were stoned and driven back."

room; its only occupant was a wounded man lying on a cot in the corner. The third room was crowded with cowering people (including Center), and so was the fourth, which looked down on the area where the police were gathered. One woman had been wounded here. The rest had escaped injury by lying on the floor; the police had been so close to the building, and their angle of fire so sharp, that they had been able to hit only those standing up. One of the men had a rifle, but he insisted that no one had returned fire from that room.

McLane and Nelson went back downstairs and asked Garrido to go up to see for himself. Garrido, now very much on the side of law and order, did so, and was easily convinced; he returned below to hold back the crowd while the passengers were sent out to join the others on the *Taboga*. He had all he could do, as did McLane and Nelson, to keep the mob from attacking and to keep his own policemen from bayoneting the Americans as they passed. Nevertheless, the riot was over. It was a little more than four hours since Jack Oliver had refused to pay a dime for a piece of watermelon.

There remained only the dreadful task of cleaning up. McLane, Nelson, and Center went back inside, turning grim and white at sight of the carnage. Among other horrors, they found a man's body with more than thirty wounds in it and a woman's body, naked except for her corsets, with the front of her thighs blackened with powder burns from a musket fired into the groin at close range. The mutilated bodies of several others lay in the freight room and on the railway tracks that led up to it. In all, there were fifteen dead, another who would die two days later, and more than fifty wounded. There were also at least three natives dead and a number wounded.

The *John L. Stephens* sailed the next morning. The natives of Panama were proud of their "victory," openly displaying the money and valuables they had stolen, bragging of the women they had raped. It was rumored that they would attack again when the *Golden Gate* arrived on Saturday, but they did not. Gradually the Isthmus sank back into lethargy; when the U.S. warships inevitably arrived at Panama and Aspinwall later that spring, it did not seem necessary to land troops to protect American interests.

The United States quickly set an official inquiry in motion under Amos Corwine, who had formerly been a consul in Panama. He found that it was "the universal opinion of respectable foreigners residing in Panama" that Miguel Habrahan was "notoriously a bad character"; more than that, he concluded that the massacre, "in view of the evidence," was the result of Habrahan's "rashness."

It was Corwine's recommendation that the United States take over and occupy the Isthmus. That opinion was shared by most of the American residents of Panama and by popular sentiment in the United States. The New York *Herald* said, "We can see no reason why the United States should not garrison Panama, Aspinwall and the line of road; ... if the precaution is neglected we may hereafter rue the neglect."

The United States did not find an appropriate way to do that until 1903, when with a show of force Theodore Roosevelt helped set up the Republic of Panama and extracted from it a permanent lease on a strip of the Isthmus suitable for a canal. In the meantime, passage across the Isthmus had to be kept free from interruption; "for this purpose, as well as for the ends of justice," wrote Secretary of State William L. Marcy, "exemplary punishment should be inflicted upon the transgressors." He did not mean Jack Oliver, of course, and certainly not the railroad management (although it was Colonel Ward's opinion that "had the railroad managers ... been a little more circumspect this unfortunate slaughter of our people would not have taken place"); and it was impossible to punish Miguel Habrahan, because he had prudently fled the country shortly after the riot. New Granada must be punished, and it was: it was ordered to pay an indemnity of $160,000.

The indemnity was eventually paid, the Panama Railroad armed all its white employees, the transit was kept open, and, for the time being, the situation simmered down. But if the periodic outbursts of the last hundred years—including the nationalistic riots in the Canal Zone in 1964—are accurate indicators, the seeds of antipathy that first bore fruit in 1856 have shown remarkable hardiness.

Mr. Kennedy lives in California and has written widely on its history. The present article is part of a forthcoming book on trans-Isthmian routes to California in the 1850's. His sources included The Panama Massacre; A Collection of the Principal Evidence and Other Documents . . . (*printed at the office of the Panama* Star and Herald, *1857*).

arbitrator. In any event, after discussing Brown's difficulty with him and his father, Buchan went to see the agents of the insurance companies; returned; discussed the situation again with Brown; and then someone—allegedly Brown—concluded that Brown should turn state's evidence, and that Buchan should arrange a deal with the insurance companies. Brown would make a complete confession and get Mrs. Hillmon to surrender the policies, while the insurance companies would take no steps to prosecute the Hillmons, Baldwin, or Brown. Buchan prepared the "confession" in the form of an affidavit:

. . . Along about the 10th day of December, 1878, John W. Hillmon, Levi Baldwin, and myself talked about and entered into a conspiracy to defraud the New York Life Insurance Company and the Mutual Life, of New York, out of some money to be obtained by means of effecting a policy or policies on the life of said John W. Hillmon. Baldwin was to furnish the money to pay the premiums . . . . Hillmon and myself were to go off southwest from Wichita, Kansas, ostensibly to locate a stock ranch, but in fact to in some way find a subject to pass off as the body of John W. Hillmon, for the purpose of obtaining the insurance money aforesaid. We had no definite plan of getting the subject. . . .

[On the 5th of March] we left [Wichita] on our second trip. . . . We overtook a stranger on this trip, the first day out from Wichita, about two or two and one half miles from town, who Hillmon invited to get in and ride, and who he (Hillmon) proposed to hire to herd and work for him on the ranch as proposed to be located. This man was with us during all this trip. Hillmon proposed to me that the man would do to pass off for him. I contended with him that the man would not do to pass off for him . . . and I protested, and said that was going beyond what we had agreed, and something I had never before thought of, and was beyond my grit entirely. But Hillmon seemed to get more deeply determined. . . . Pains were taken not to have more than two of us seen together in the wagon. . . . Hillmon kept at the man until he let him vaccinate him, which he did, taking his pocket knife and using virus from his own arm for the purpose. He also traded clothes with him. . . . This man appeared to be a stranger in the country, a sort of an easy-go-long fellow, not suspicious or very attentive to anything. His arm became very sore, and he got quite stupid and dull. He said his name was either Berkley or Burgess, or something sounding like that. We always called him Joe. He said he had been around Fort Scott awhile, and also had worked about Wellington or Arkansas City. I do not know where he was from, nor where his home or friends were. I did not see him at Wichita that I know of. I had but very little to say to the man, and less to do with him. . . . I frequently remonstrated with Hillmon, and tried to deter him from carrying out his intentions of killing the man.

The next evening after we got to the camp last named [on Crooked Creek], the man Joe was sitting by the fire. I was at the hind end of the wagon, either putting feed in the box for the horses or taking a sack of corn out, when I heard a gun go off. I looked around, and saw the man was shot, and Hillmon was pulling him away around to keep him out of the fire. Hillmon changed a daybook from his own coat to Joe's, and said to me everything was all right, and that I need not be afraid. . . . He told me to get a pony . . . and get some one to come up. He took Joe's valise, and started north. . . . I have never heard a word from him since. . . .

I make the above statements in the Hillmon case as the full and true facts in the case, regretting the part I have taken in the affair.

Brown executed and swore to this affidavit on the fourth of September, 1879. At the same time he gave Buchan written authority "to make arrangements, if he can, with the insurance companies for a settlement of the Hillmon case, by them stopping all pursuit and prosecution of myself and John W. Hillmon, if suit for money is stopped and policies surrendered to companies."

Then began a period of correspondence and visits between Brown and Sallie Hillmon. He first had a midnight rendezvous with her at Baldwin's house, told her what he had done, and got her to meet Buchan. She did so on several occasions—and once stayed at Buchan's home at Wyandotte for three weeks. She was always in need of funds, and did not hesitate to ask him for train tickets or money that she could not get from Baldwin. In September she wrote Buchan from Ottawa, Kansas, that:

. . . it will never do for you to come to my sisters. I will tell you the reason when I see you. . . . I will be obleged to ask you to send me enough to bye my Ticket to your city. . . . I did write that letter to Riggs & Borgholthaus [her attorneys] have got no answer and don't want any.

I will be on the Wendsday's Train without something offle happens.

In September, 1880, Sallie gave Buchan a full "release" of all her interest in the insurance policies; but she did not have the policies themselves. They were in the hands of Baldwin's lawyer, who refused to give them up, saying he had a lien on them for $10,000. Buchan showed her Brown's statement and the agreement of the companies not to prosecute him; but then, somehow—perhaps at her insistence—Brown's statement got torn up and dropped into a stove. (Later, when negotiations with her finally broke off, it was remembered that the stove was unlighted, and the pieces of the statement were fished out and preserved.)

The situation grew more and more puzzling. Despite all her friendly visits with Buchan, Sallie evidently never made any statements of fact that were inconsistent with her previous claims, or contrary to any of her testimony in the case. If she had, Buchan was not the man to have kept it secret. Indeed, it may be just as likely that Sallie was playing a game with Buchan as that he was spinning a web for her. The fact is that Buchan got no further results. The policies were not surrendered. Sallie's "release" had no legal effect. Only Brown's statement, rescued from the fireless stove, took its place among the mass of evidence served up to six juries. But soon after Sallie filed her suit and it became clear that he was in no real danger of criminal prosecution, Brown—can it surprise you?—repudiated his "confession" and reverted to his original story. With not unreasonable caution, Sallie's lawyers took Brown's deposition before the case came on for trial, and had him repeat his original story of how he had accidentally shot Hillmon. The insurance lawyers cross-examined him for nineteen days, but they were unable to get him back to the tale he had told in his written "confession."

Up to this point the insurance companies' conclusion that there had been a conspiracy was based on their own natural suspicions, the odd remarks of Levi Baldwin, and the written "confession" of Brown. As late as the summer of 1879 they thought the body was that of one Frank Nichols, who had disappeared from Wichita; but he turned up. Then perseverance and luck brought them evidence concerning another person whose description might fit the dead body.

In Fort Madison, Iowa, there lived the parents, the sisters, and the sweetheart of a young German named Frederick Adolph Walters. Fred had left that town to seek his fortune about a year before the occurrence on Crooked Creek. During this year he had wandered around Missouri, Iowa, Nebraska, and Kansas, spending time in various towns, including Wichita. On the first of

March, 1879, a few days before Hillmon and Brown left on their final trip, Walters wrote his sister a letter from Wichita:

I in my usual style, will drop you a few lines to let you know that I intend leaving Wichita on or about March 5th, with a certain Mr. Hillmon, a sheep trader, for Colorado, and parts unknown to me. . . .

At about the same time he wrote his sweetheart, Alvina Kasten, a longer letter dated March 1, 1879:

Dearest Alvina:

. . . I will stay here until the fore part of next week, and then will leave here to see part of the country which I never expected to see when I left home, as I am going with a man by the name of Hillmon, who intends to start a sheep ranch, and as he promised me more wages than I could make at anything else, I concluded to take it for a while, at least until I struck something better. There is so many folks in this country that have got the Leadville [mining] fever, and if I would not have got the situation that I have now, I would of went there myself; but as it is at present, I will get to see the best part of Kansas, Indian Territory, Colorado and New Mexico. The route that we intend to take would cost a man to travel from $150 to $200, but it will not cost me a cent; besides I get good wages. I will drop you a letter occasionally until I get settled down, then I want you to answer it (you bet, honey).

Thereafter time passed without further letters to sweetheart, sister, or family, though previously Fred Walters' letters in "usual style" had been steady and regular. When his new silence extended into weeks and months, the family became alarmed and began to make inquiries. The inquiries eventually came to Lawrence, and from there someone sent the family photographs of the controversial dead body. These they immediately declared to be pictures of the missing Walters. There was even a mole on the back of the dead body in just the place where the new witnesses swore Walters had had a mole. To be sure, his sister said that he had had a scar on his ankle, received from a dog bite when he was twelve years old; the doctors' minute examination of the dead body in Lawrence had revealed no ankle scars, but the scar might have disappeared over the years.

The Hillmon case was now popularly reduced to a single question: Was the dead body Hillmon or Walters? There were several difficulties with the Walters theory. All the testimony identifying the body as Walters was based on photographs of a weeks-old corpse with a burned face. Apart from such identification there was nothing to connect Walters with Hillmon and Brown except the letters to his girl friend and his sister. No one was ever produced who had seen Walters with Hillmon or Brown, or who had seen Walters near Crooked Creek or Medicine Lodge. And if Brown's "confession" is referred to, there is nothing in it that is completely consistent with the Walters letters. If Hillmon hired Walters in Wichita, either he did not tell Brown about it or Brown's "confession" was not forthright. The name "Berkley or Burgess" which Brown cited in his statement is certainly not "Walters"; "Joe" is not a likely nickname for "Frederick Adolph"; and the travels that Brown ascribed to Joe do not correspond with the known travels of Walters.

So the letters from Wichita were the only real support of the Walters theory. Their genuineness was not questioned, and the inferences drawn from them seemed inescapable in the light of Walters' complete disappearance. Sallie's attorneys tried to destroy the effect of the letters in two ways—factually (by pointing out to the jurors that Hillmon was a very common name in Kansas and that the letters did not say "John Hillmon") and legally (by objecting that the letters were "hearsay" and as such inadmissible in evidence).

For at least two centuries the rule against hearsay has been one of the foundation stones of the law of evidence. Indeed, about the time of the Hillmon case, an Alabama court declared that this rule had been one of the rights guaranteed to Englishmen by the Magna Charta. This was more than a slight historical error, but it showed the reverence that courts and lawyers have had for the rule. Chancellor James Kent, the author of America's first great law book, gave this reason for the rule against hearsay:

A person who relates a hearsay is not obliged to enter into any particulars, to answer any questions, to solve any difficulties, to reconcile any contradictions, to explain any obscurities, to remove any ambiguities; he entrenches himself in the simple assertion that he was told so, and leaves the burden entirely on his dead or absent author.

Popular faith in the cross-questioning of witnesses was expressed by the commercial Mr. Moulder, in Anthony Trollope's *Orley Farm:* "It is the fairest thing that is. It's the bulwark of the British Constitution. Trial by jury is, and how can you have trial by jury if the witnesses are not to be cross-questioned?"

There are and always have been exceptions to the hearsay rule, to allow for statements made by one who cannot be in court for questioning but who is nonetheless presumed to have told the truth—deathbed statements, or routine business entries, or confessions of something which it would be to his interest not to confess. But Walters' letters were not his dying declarations, though his doom may already have been sealed when he wrote them; they were not confessions or admissions of anything that Walters could have been expected to want to conceal. The insurance lawyers argued that the letters were a kind of business entry;

but a man's business ought not to include his love letters.

The legal question was not resolved for twelve years. At the first trial, in 1882, the letters were admitted in evidence, despite objection; but the jury disagreed seven to five, and no verdict resulted. So the case was retried in 1885, with the same result, except that the division in the jury was six to six. On the third trial, in 1888, Judge O. P. Shiras refused to admit the letters in evidence, and then the jury brought in a full verdict for Sal-

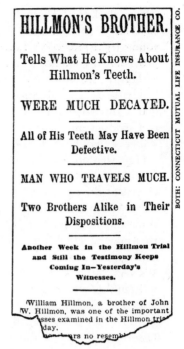

lie Hillmon for the amount of the policies plus accumulated interest. The defendants appealed to the United States Supreme Court; and the Kansas state superintendent of insurance (who had been of counsel for the insurance companies in the second trial) included in his annual report a full account of the evidence in the case, reporting that which had been admitted by the court and some which had not, and adding comments of his own, mostly favorable to the companies. (This report, as republished in *The Principles of Judicial Proof* by the late, great writer on the law of evidence John Henry Wigmore, is the principal authority for many of the statements in the present account.)

In the first hearing before the Supreme Court, in 1892, the insurance-company attorneys apparently presented no sound theory by which the Walters letters could have been held admissible, and we are told that the point was "miserably argued." Nevertheless, the Supreme Court justices voted unanimously to decide in favor of the insurance companies on general principles, thus reversing the lower-court findings and clearing the way for a new trial.

The preparation of the Supreme Court's opinion was assigned to Justice Horace Gray, who could be relied upon to find a precedent for the decision if anyone could do so. He was the most learned and resourceful member of the court—a Harvard graduate, a former chief justice of Massachusetts, an heir to wealth, and a thorough Bostonian. Typically, his opinions were larded with judicial citations and legal principles. Yet we are reliably told that even he was in "dense darkness" about how to justify the admission of Walters' letters, until a suggestion came from his young legal secretary's father, James Bradley Thayer, professor of evidence at the Harvard Law School. Together Justice Gray and Thayer brought forth a new legal theory and adorned it with their authority. A man's intention, they said—whenever that intention is a distinct and material fact in a chain of circumstances—may be proved by his own contemporaneous oral or written declarations. For truly, how better can we find out what a man thinks than by what he does or says at the time? And was not Walters' intention to leave Wichita with Hillmon the sheep trader a distinct and material fact in the chain of circumstances that may have led him to Crooked Creek? To be sure, as the professor knew, no court would have allowed Walters' letter to be admitted in evidence if he had written his sweetheart, saying, "I have left Wichita with Hillmon the sheep trader." Such a letter would indisputably have been hearsay. But the learned professor suggested that there was a logical difference between a hearsay account of a past fact and Walters' personal expression of his then present intent; the Supreme Court agreed.

Justice Gray's opinion (Insurance Company v. Hillmon, 145 U.S. 285) is famous among lawyers. Generations of them have debated whether such a distinction between a past fact and a present intention is sound or unsound. Forty years later, Justice Benjamin Cardozo, speaking for the Supreme Court in Franklin Roosevelt's day, said the decision in the Hillmon case "marks the high water line beyond which courts have been unwilling to go."

But the legal points of the decision were lost on the Kansas public of the nineties. To them the real question was one of motive: Who was being made the victim of conspiracy—the insurance companies or the Kansas widow? These were the years of full flood for the People's party in Kansas and the Midwest. One Mary "Yellin" Lease rode all over the middle border, telling the farmers that "Wall Street owns the country" and urging them to "raise less corn and more hell." At their first national convention—in Omaha on the Fourth of July, 1892—the Populists declared:

We meet in the midst of a nation brought to the verge of moral, political and material ruin. Corruption dominates the ballot-box, the Legislatures, the Congress and touches even the ermine of the bench. . . . From the same prolific womb of governmental injustice we breed the two great classes—tramps and millionaires.

To those Kansans who followed the Populists, the Hillmon case was a heroic contest between the wealth of Wall Street and a poor, defenseless widow of Kansas whose cause involved the very good name of the state itself. They had no more faith in the motives and ways of the insurance companies than the companies had in Hillmon. Wealth had paid the doctors to lose Hillmon's vaccination scab; wealth had paid Buchan to extort a false confession from Brown and to deceive Sallie; and in everything the hand of wealth and influence was fashioning a crown of thorns and a cross of gold for one poor, weak, bereaved woman. When the insurance companies persuaded one of Hillmon's old girl friends and his sister and brother-in-law to take the witness stand to testify that Hillmon had a blackened or missing front tooth and not, like the corpse, a perfect set of teeth, those with Populist leanings called the brother-in-law a wretch and the girl friend a spiteful old maid, and accused the insurance companies of buying their false testimony.

Sallie's lawyers scorned the defense's accusations. "Such a conspiracy as the defense alleges must [if true] result in lasting separation from his young wife —the blighting of both their lives forever—her lifelong misery and his eternal damnation." If, they said, the arguments of the insurance lawyers were to be believed, "Hillmon must have been a marvelous man. One of a party of three, traveling through a settled country, camping out, and stopping at houses, he succeeded in concealing one of the party through the entire journey from Wichita to Medicine Lodge. Not only that, but he vaccinated him, made it work, kept the protesting Brown at bay, and succeeds in his conspiracy." Finally—and mark you—"These insurance companies with boundless wealth and inexhaustible resources at their command, with agents scattered the world over, with . . . years to operate in, have failed to find Hillmon. . . . With all their money and all their power they have never been able to find a vestige of Hillmon."

Defending themselves against this sort of attack, the insurance companies at first hinted that Hillmon's whereabouts were known to the authorities, and that it would be only a matter of time before he would be produced. When time passed and he was not brought forth, they pictured him as a "typical Western bravo," and it was "surmised that the detectives are more afraid of him than desirous of getting the reward for his capture." But no one ever found Hillmon.

Walters never showed up either; but Sallie's lawyers had no difficulty in explaining that they never had the money and the resources to search for *him*.

Between 1892 and 1897 two more trials were held (the fourth and fifth of the series) and two more juries

Mr. Maccracken, who is a lawyer in Cleveland, was the author of "Althea and the Judges" in our June, 1967, issue.

disagreed. In 1897, when the Populists were in control of the Kansas state administration, Sallie's lawyers took a new tack; and Webb McNall, as superintendent of insurance, denied Mutual Life a license to continue to do business in Kansas, because "I am satisfied that your company has not dealt fairly with the plaintiff, Mrs. Sallie E. Hillmon, in refusing to pay the death loss and in the litigation of the same pertaining to her deceased husband." When this came to the attention of federal judge John A. Williams, who had presided at the fifth trial, he promptly had a federal grand jury bring in an indictment against the superintendent of insurance for interference with the rights of litigants in his court, and on the petition of the insurance company he issued a mandatory injunction against both the superintendent and the attorney general of Kansas, enjoining them from interfering in the insurance company's transaction of business in Kansas. Apparently no one actually went to prison, but the insurance companies continued in business. By this time New York Life had thought it wise to settle with Sallie Hillmon, but the other two, Mutual Life and Connecticut Mutual, continued to contest the case.

The sixth trial began in October, 1899. In the course of it the trial judge surprised the defense by ruling that Brown's "confession" of conspiracy against the insurance companies, and Baldwin's conspiratorial remarks about Hillmon, dead bodies, and insurance, were not proper evidence against Sallie since she was not charged with being a party to the conspiracy. This ruling so weakened the case for the insurance companies that the jury brought in a verdict for the plaintiff. Mutual Life then gave up the battle and paid; but Connecticut Mutual made 108 assignments of error and appealed. The circuit court of appeals affirmed the trial court, but on further appeal the Supreme Court, in 1903, again reversed the judgment and ordered a new trial.

The opinion was written by Justice Henry Billings Brown of Michigan. He had had the misfortune of losing the sight of one eye shortly after he was appointed to the court in 1890, but with his good eye he had no trouble seeing that the "widow" stood to benefit from the conspiracy whether she was a party to it or not, and in his view the whole case was simply one of "graveyard insurance." (Even the annual premiums of $600 for the life insurance were more than Hillmon had ever earned in a year.) This time, however, the court was not unanimous. Two of the justices dissented—Justice (later Chief Justice) Edward White of Louisiana and Justice David Brewer of Kansas, who had himself presided at the second trial and was presumably more intimately familiar with the case than any of the justices. They wrote no dissenting opinion,

but perhaps they agreed with the words of the circuit judge, Amos M. Thayer:

This case has been pending...for more than 21 years, and it would be a matter of great regret, and a reproach to our method of administering justice if, after six laborious and lengthy trials, an error had crept into the record of such consequence as to require reversal.

In any event, a seventh trial was then too much to contemplate even for the parties themselves; and a settlement with the last of the insurance companies was finally reached. (Counting accumulated interest, the "widow" eventually received a total of $35,700 from the three companies.) She had been for some years happily remarried, with no apparent apprehensions of bigamy; and whether or not her *sang-froid* was justified, it would not be too long before a future Chief Justice of the United States, Charles Evans Hughes, would gain first fame by his investigation of New York life insurance scandals.

The truth in the Hillmon case is as debatable today as it was when it began. Some twenty years after the last court decision the dean of Kansas journalists, T. A. McNeal, in a book of reminiscences, *When Kansas Was Young*, would express the novel opinion that Hillmon did conspire to defraud the insurance companies, but that something went wrong and he was really killed at Crooked Creek. McNeal is entitled to respect because he began his newspaper career on the Medicine Lodge *Cresset* in the spring of 1879, just after the first inquest; and if in the next fifty years or so either Hillmon or Walters had ever been heard from, McNeal would have reported it. However, his little book does not reveal how or why he came to his odd conclusion.

You now have all the facts and theories that are known; perhaps the best way to conclude is with the words with which Justice Brewer, a son, grandson, and nephew of clergymen, concluded his charge to the jury in the second trial:

Consider all the facts in the case. Fear not. Be just; and may that infinite Being, who from His unseen throne in the center of this mystic universe, who sees and knows the very fact, help you to be strong and guide you to truth.

courthouse, hoping to find Revolutionary War documents. He found instead the long-lost 1771 marriage license bond of Thomas Jefferson and Martha Skelton of Charles City County. It had been wrapped in a bundle of papers and overlooked for decades.

The next morning Lossing drove into Sherwood Forest, former President Tyler's estate. Tyler greeted him warmly and urged him to stay for an extended visit. But time was precious; what Lossing really wanted was directions to Jamestown. The former Chief Executive drew a rough map. Unfortunately, it did not show the wretched state of the roads through the surrounding swamps and failed to note that the ferry across the nearby Chickahominy River had been abandoned. Two men cleaned out a decrepit scow, loaded Lossing, Charley, and the dearborn aboard, and took them across the Chickahominy, bailing as they went.

Williamsburg's creeping ruin saddened Lossing. Old Bruton Parish Church and the octagonal powder magazine on the green remained intact, but most of the village was deteriorating. Lord Dunmore's palace, home of Virginia's royal governors, was blackened by fire. It happened that carpenters were just then remodelling the Raleigh Tavern, scene of anti-British gatherings before the Revolution. "Up to the day of my visit it had remained unaltered," Lossing wrote. His notes and sketches were to help in the twentieth-century restoration.

He reached Yorktown at twilight on December 20 and put up at the town's only inn, the Swan Tavern, run by William Nelson, grandson of Governor Thomas Nelson, one of the signers of the Declaration of Independence. The next day Nelson took him across what Lossing called Lord Cornwallis' "field of humiliation." The visitor went into "Cornwallis' Cave," allegedly the spot where the British general had held councils of war. Lossing reluctantly paid twelve and a half cents admission, "knowing that I was submitting to imposition." He sketched the battlefield within sight of Governor Nelson's home. In his drawing the British works appeared surprisingly well preserved after nearly seventy years.

Yorktown may have been a disappointment, for Lossing found no one closer to the scenes of October, 1781, than Nelson. He left and spent Christmas Day in Norfolk to the sound of "guns, pistols and squibs heralding the holiday." Later he stopped to see Jefferson's home, Monticello, and found it "deprived of its former beauty by neglect." Now he swung southwestward into North Carolina, to Guilford Courthouse near Greensboro; southwest again to Charlotte and west to Cowpens, South Carolina. Roads were bad or non-existent through the swamps and the slashes. Rivers had to be forded, often at full flood. Lossing feared that he might lose his hundreds of sketches and his stack of notebooks. He slept where he could: one night in a mansion, the next in a forest hut, another in a post office or run-down tavern. He ate whatever the area offered, as pleased with a sandwich as with a sumptuous meal at a good inn along the way.

He was reliving the days of 1780 and 1781 when Marion, Sumter, and Greene stalked this wild country, fending off the British and Tories led by Ferguson, Arnold, and Cornwallis. He climbed mountains, rode saddle horses, drove Charley over nearly impassable roads, ever following the quest. The Poughkeepsie pilgrim entered Camden, South Carolina, on January 18, 1849, after driving Charley fourteen hundred miles in sixty-two days. He then sold the faithful horse and took a train for Savannah to catch a ship north. He reached New York on February 4, 1849, and "sat by my own fireside," pleased that he had suffered neither sickness nor accident.

Lossing rapidly transformed his notes into a huge manuscript of more than seven hundred thousand words, including a wealth of fascinating footnotes that ranged from obscure little poems to explanations of his drawings. He turned his rough field sketches into finished renderings, each the size it would be in the book. He prepared the index, laid out the pages, read the proofs, wrote letters seeking more information or submitting proofs (as he did to Longfellow), and drew handsome initial letters for each chapter. Moreover, he personally transformed most of his renderings into wood engravings. On the basis of sheer volume of work, it was a magnificent achievement.

The *Pictorial Field-Book of the Revolution* began appearing in July, 1850, in monthly "parts" (small paperback books) and continued until thirty were issued. Simultaneously, a large two-volume edition was prepared. Volume I appeared in 1851, carrying readers through the Boston trip. Volume II was ready a year later. The two totalled more than 1,450 pages and contained about 1,100 woodcuts.

The *Field-Book* sold well, and ultimately three editions appeared. Lossing was acclaimed wherever history buffs met, even though some of the nation's small band of professional historians protested that his journalistic approach sacrificed academic standards on the altar of popularity. Lossing savored the accolades, welcomed the mass of correspondence coming into his Poughkeepsie parlors, and enjoyed a mounting interchange of ideas with historians all over the nation.

Requests for his services flowed in. *Harper's Magazine* used his self-illustrated articles, covering a wide range of topics, nearly every month during the 1850's and also employed him to illustrate contributions by others. The second Mrs. Lossing—his first wife died in 1855—accompanied her husband into the Adirondack wilds to do research for a series of articles that appeared in 1860 and 1861 in the London *Art-Journal*. These were later pulled together into one volume, *The Hudson, from the Wilderness to the Sea,* published in 1866.

The Hudson is one of Lossing's most charming books. He and his wife had followed Indian guides over rocky, unmarked trails to reach the spot where the river rises, then traced the Hudson's course to New York City. Lossing worked strictly as a journalist, interviewing natives, collecting facts, and weaving the whole into a readable text illustrated with his art.

Lossing had ended his *Pictorial Field-Book of the Revolution* by promising that "should time deal gently with us, we may again go out with staff and scrip together upon the great highway of our country's progress, to note the march of events there." His hope to do for the War of 1812 what he had done for the Revolution was delayed by an intensive schedule that did not permit much travel until 1860. Then he was off, his expenses again underwritten by Harper's.

 He wrote about this war chronologically rather than as a series of trips to important sites. This technique probably made the work more acceptable to scholars, but although well written the book lacked the vigor and flavor of the *Field-Book of the Revolution*. No personal experiences were related until page 195; there the *Pictorial Field-Book of the War of 1812* picked up pace, for Lossing was a lively reporter.

He was in Indianapolis on September 28, 1860, a day when "Judge Douglas, one of the candidates for the Presidency" was to speak at a county fair. Before noon, more than twenty thousand people were jammed into that growing frontier city. Lossing saw Douglas, but, once more marching to the beat of an earlier drum, passed up a chance to hear him speak and took the midday train to Terre Haute. (Safely aboard, he found that his pocket had been picked by an Indianapolis sharpster.)

In the course of ten thousand miles of travel, Lossing met veterans who had served under William Henry Harrison at Tippecanoe and old sailors who had trod the decks of ships under Oliver Hazard Perry. He had dinner with three hundred War of 1812 veterans in Cleveland on September 10, 1860, when a statue of Perry was dedicated. Lossing figured that the aggregate age of the veterans was "about 20,000 years." The oldest was Abraham Chase, a ninety-year-old Negro. Two of the veterans were "only fifty-seven"; they had been "boys in the service."

Lossing crisscrossed the region near the Great Lakes and travelled up and down the East Coast. In Bangor, Maine, he talked with Henry Van Meter, "a remarkable black man, then ninety-five years of age." Van Meter had been a slave of Virginia's Governor Nelson during the Revolution and said he had seen George Washington many times. After the Revolution the slave escaped to freedom and served as a sailor aboard the privateer *Lawrence* in 1814.

Lossing had one last trip to make: the book could not be complete without a visit to New Orleans. Despite a warning letter from "a distinguished South Carolina author to defer my visit," Lossing travelled west in the first week of April, 1861, through burntout Harpers Ferry and thence south through Kentucky to the lower Mississippi.

General H. W. Palfrey, who had been a participant in the Battle of New Orleans in 1814, promised to lead him over the battleground on April 12. That day the telegraph carried news of the attack on Fort Sumter, and Palfrey pleaded that he was "too busy with public matters." Lossing went on his own, aware that as his research on one war was ending, another war was beginning. As he toured the grounds he heard the firing of victory cannon in New Orleans and remarked to his driver, "Fort Sumter is doubtless gone." He returned to a joyous city "alive with excitement" and pleased to be at war.

Out on the streets, troops drilled in their distinctive corps garb, many of them in the Zouave uniforms that were also popular with Northern units. Citizens wore "secession rosettes," and small Confederate flags fluttered from most windows. Enthusiasm diminished, however, on April 15, when bulletin boards carried the news that President Lincoln had called for seventy-five thousand soldiers. In the face of that, people "turned thoughtful." Lossing commented: ". . . war would ruin the business of New Orleans." As he left the city on April 17, he saw Negroes "quietly at work in the fields, planting cotton, little dreaming of their redemption from Slavery being so nigh." He was deluding himself that this would be a short struggle.

Passing through one Confederate stronghold after another, Lossing heard dire rumors: that Massachusetts troops had been attacked and routed in Baltimore, that Harpers Ferry had been occupied by Secessionists, that General Winfield Scott had "resigned his commission and offered his services to Virginia—and that President Lincoln was about to follow his example." Cut off from the Union side of the news, the historian was alarmed.

He felt immense relief when he crossed the Ohio River to Cincinnati. There were American flags flying everywhere, and young men crowded the railroad cars on their way to camp. From the car windows he could see soldiers drilling in the moonlight. Pittsburgh was "more noisy with the drum than with the tilt-hammer." Philadelphia was "gay and brilliant with the ensigns of war." New York was "a vast military camp." Lossing's fears were far behind him.

The *Pictorial Field-Book of the War of 1812* had to be set aside when interest at Harper's lessened because of the Civil War. Eventually Lossing finished the 400,000 words of text and prepared 882 illustrations; Harper's published it in 1868.

Meanwhile, Lossing knew that he could not wait until participants in the Civil War became old men. He would gather material as the war progressed and be ready as soon as peace came. President Lincoln, Secretary of War Edwin M. Stanton, and Secretary of the Navy Gideon Welles gave him carte blanche through Union lines, and he bore letters of introduction to nearly every important Union officer.

Yet in the course of the war it was difficult to visit any theatre of battle. Lossing made only two major excursions during the fighting, both anticlimactic: he surveyed the Gettysburg battlefield a week after the struggle there; and, from the deck of a Union ship, he watched an abortive attack on Fort Fisher, North Carolina, in December, 1864.

In any case, George W. Childs of Philadelphia, Lossing's new publisher, rushed Volume I of the *Pictorial History of the Civil War* (later renamed *Pictorial Field-Book of the Civil War*) into print in 1866. Lossing tried to make up for having seen little of the action by extended postwar visits to the South, to gather enough data and illustrations for two more volumes.

Between March 27 and June 10, 1866, he went from Fort Fisher to Savannah, across Georgia to New Orleans, up the Mississippi to Vicksburg, and then back to Nashville, Chattanooga, Atlanta, Richmond, through the Virginia Peninsula, and into the Wilderness. It was a typical fast-moving Lossing dash, up at dawn and full speed all day. From the train window he saw ruined railway stations, twisted iron rails, and charred ties tracing General William T. Sherman's march to the sea. Atlanta already showed "signs of

resurrection," although everywhere "rank vines were creeping over heaps of brick and stone."

Steaming up the Alabama River to Selma, Lossing was assailed by "three or four young women" who "uttered many bitter words, in a high key, about the 'Yankees' . . . intended for our special hearing." He rebuked their "ill breeding by kindness and courtesy," and before the trip ended, the "estimate each had set upon the other" was changed for the better.

After struggling all day through the marshes near Shiloh, Lossing accepted an invitation from a widow to spend a night in one of her desolate cabins near the battlefield. She had lived on the edge of Shiloh during the battle in April, 1862. A shell went through her house but she, her consumptive husband, and their six children had all escaped injury. The traveller nailed his horse into a room in the log cabin that night, fearful that roaming bushwhackers might steal the animal.

Lossing travelled from Nashville down the Cumberland River early in May aboard a steamer loaded with two hundred discharged Negro soldiers. Frightened white passengers ("mostly Secessionists") made plans, in case of a riot, to surrender the boat to the Negroes "on demand," after rejecting a proposal to shower the troops with hot water from the boiler. Lossing said that the fears were ridiculous: he "never saw a more orderly and well-disposed company of men, just loosed from military discipline, than they."

Time after time on this journey, Lossing met chaplains and soldiers assigned to bury the dead still on the fields, or to transfer bodies of fallen men who had been interred in hastily dug and poorly marked graves. This was the beginning of the national cemeteries throughout the South. He was moved by "the whitened bones" of many soldiers in shallow graves in the woods.

The historical research was prodigious. Quite aside from his travels, Lossing spent long weeks poring over both Confederate and Union records. He conscientiously interviewed participants and spectators from both sides. The completed Civil War history ran to three thick volumes, each averaging about 625 pages

Mr. Cunningham recently completed a term as president of the New Jersey Historical Society. He is the author of several books, including New Jersey: America's Main Road *(Doubleday, 1966), a history of the state. He did much of his research for this article at the Henry E. Huntington Library in San Marino, California.*

with about 400 illustrations. When Childs decided not to publish beyond the first book, volumes II and III were brought out in 1868 by Thomas Belknap of Hartford. For the first time, Lossing used the sketches of others to supplement the hundreds that he drew for the books. Much of his personal travel story appeared in footnotes describing his own sketches.

Lossing was now at his peak of popularity, busier and more in demand than ever. He maintained a great interest in his own Dutchess County in New York. In 1861 he had become one of the founding trustees of Vassar Female College, and he kept active in college affairs until his death. One of his more vehement correspondents was Mrs. Sarah Hale of Philadelphia, editor of *Godey's Lady's Book,* who urged him to omit the word "female" from the college name. Her campaign succeeded. In 1866, Lossing asked his colleagues, "Who ever heard of a *male* college? . . . Why not Yale Male College or Harvard Male University?" The other trustees agreed; the offending word was dropped. A year later, the trustees wanted a history of Vassar College written, and assigned the honorary task to Lossing. He fitted the chore between hours spent on his Civil War study and produced a handsome book before the June commencement in 1867.

Lossing moved in 1869 to a 350-acre farm on a high hill near Dover Plains, about twenty miles east of Poughkeepsie. By 1872 his family of two sons and two daughters was complete. He attached a two-story library and study to the old frame farmhouse at The Ridge. There he started work long before breakfast, wrote or studied until lunch, then went back to work until late-afternoon tea.

His study became hopelessly cluttered, since Lossing saved everything—notebooks, originals of his sketches, the manuscripts of books and articles, proof sheets, thousands of letters, pamphlets, pictures, and scraps of paper filled with memoranda. But production never lapsed. By 1890 he had written and published more than forty historical and biographical books, plus hundreds of magazine and newspaper articles. His own published illustrations ran well upwards of ten thousand pieces. Several of his later books were illustrated by his daughter Helen.

Life was pleasant, if not exciting. Friends might come to visit, or the Lossings might go to a statue unveiling or a cemetery dedication. One firm friend from Civil War days was General Lew Wallace, who called at The Ridge while he was writing *Ben Hur* to discuss historical backgrounds with Lossing. Honors came his way. Nothing pleased him more than the LL.D. bestowed on him by the University of Michigan in 1872.

Lossing died suddenly at The Ridge on June 3,

1891, after a one-day illness. Even as letters of condolence poured in, some contemporaries began to question his stature as a historian. His critics said that he had not weighed both sides of the Revolution; they forgot that British papers were not available when he made his travels in 1848. A few questioned the sheer volume of his writing, as if to suggest that a high output automatically made the work's authenticity suspect. Some downgraded the soundness of Lossing's research, obviously not aware of his painstaking correspondence with far-flung authorities that questioned even the slightest details before publication. If he had erred, it was not through negligence.

As for the interviews with Revolutionary veterans, whose testimony many claimed to be nothing more than hearsay or folklore, Lossing never saw them as either completely accurate or important in themselves. He carefully attributed his subjects' utterances, and sometimes questioned their memories. It was interesting material, not necessarily vital—it was meant to lure readers into history.

Left behind in the old farmhouse when he died was an amazing mass of historical and personal materials. Mrs. Lossing died in 1911 and the three surviving children asked the Anderson Galleries in New York to catalogue the holdings and offer them for sale. A representative of the firm reported in astonishment that he found trunks filled with more than thirty thousand letters, many signed by leading figures of the nineteenth century. He came upon valuable pamphlets, maps, prints, manuscripts, and documents stuffed in cupboards. The original manuscripts of all Lossing's books, plus his field sketches and hundreds of finished drawings, were on shelves or in boxes.

The first Lossing material went on sale in May, 1912, and there were more than a dozen auctions over a period of about eight years before the amazing collection was scattered. Fortunately, a great deal of the material was acquired by the Henry E. Huntington Library, including most of Lossing's handwritten manuscripts, hundreds of letters, and several boxes filled with original drawings.

Regardless of how Benson J. Lossing is ranked as a historian, this much is certain: if he could have known in June, 1848, where those steps in Horse Neck, Connecticut, would lead, he would still unhesitatingly have reined his horse to a halt. For Lossing, eyewitnesses to history and their tales made life worth the living. And always, around any corner, there might be another who had seen history pass.

ALL: *Field-Book of the War of 1812*

Pulitzer and His "Indegoddampendent" Editor

CONTINUED FROM PAGE 21

ning the editorial page, a month at a time, alternating with the milder-mannered John L. Heaton under Merrill's fatherly eye. "Mr. P. agreed to be patient of blunders," a memorandum about the arrangement concludes ominously, "if Mr. Cobb would be patient of criticism"—a large order either way. Mr. P. soon upset this routine, first by giving Merrill a long vacation, then by easing him out, and from time to time by depriving Cobb of his monthly turn, the worst punishment he could inflict.

Each August came the dreaded invitation from Chatwold, the Pulitzer estate at Bar Harbor. During these visits the blind man sought to pick his editor's brains, instruct him, and chart the *World*'s course. J. P. functioned best while in motion, either astride a favorite mount with his editor at his side, his watchful groom following, or cruising about the coves of Frenchman Bay in his big electric launch. He would pull news clippings, editorials, and memoranda from his pockets, thrust them at Cobb for reading, question him sharply, and then deliver a torrent of comment. When they got home he usually ordered his editor to write a report of the points he had made, to be certain they had penetrated. *World* editors and executives tended to pale at mention of Bar Harbor.

Whatever these visits did to the editor, in February of 1906 he wrote Pulitzer that the owners of the Detroit *Free Press* had offered him carte blanche and a piece of the paper to get him back, and that the offer was too good to refuse. This was in the mail to Jekyll Island when a telegram from there crossed it: "HAVE JUST READ WEDNESDAY'S CRAZY PAGE AND IT HAS MADE ME SICK." Cobb had run a slashing attack on New York's Rapid Transit Board. It was, said Pulitzer, a splendid board; Cobb must run "a double-leaded paragraph expressing regret for your intemperance of language." Cobb did nothing of the kind. As soon as J. P. returned to New York, the editor sent him a one-sentence letter in an envelope marked "Personal and Immediate." It was as terse as Pulitzer could ask:

Dear Mr. Pulitzer:
I hereby tender you my resignation to take immediate effect.
Respectfully yours,
Frank I. Cobb

An urgent call on the private line from the Pulitzer mansion on Seventy-third Street fetched Seitz, and the two set out for a drive in Central Park in a snowstorm —a measure of J. P.'s agitation, for normally he would not venture outdoors without at least one secretary's

weather report. What to do about Cobb? The bluff, pugnacious Seitz had grown fond of Cobb as a man after his own heart. (A typical J. P. telegram upbraiding *him* had come to his desk a few days before with an impish line added in Cobb's hand—"Now will you be good?") Still, Seitz saw no use in holding Cobb to his contract against his will, and said so. Pulitzer held his peace. The carriage completed its circuit. As it reached the Seventy-second Street exit he said quietly, "I liked that young man. I liked the way he swore." The carriage turned up Fifth Avenue, half a block from home. Suddenly, in a voice full of fury that Seitz could never forget: "Go back to the office and tell that goddamned young fool I will *not* let him resign, goddamn him!"

Cobb took the news with a grin. Two days later J. P. came through with another raise, adding, by way of trying for the last word, that this was to be considered an inducement for better editorial writing. There were no last words between these two. Cobb gave Pulitzer to understand, in thanking him when the next raise came, that money was no object. "My tastes are rather simple," he wrote. "What I care most about money is not having to think about it."

Where did the *World* stand, in these years of its glory? Perhaps a paragraph from a Cobb editorial sums it up as well as anything can:

There is seldom more than one vital issue in American politics—government for Privilege *versus* government for the People. That is the beginning and end of the trust question, of the tariff question, of the financial question, of the conservation question, of the boss question.

On the equally vital issue of individual liberty versus a strong central government, the paper veered, like conservatives today, toward liberty. Pulitzer had no use for states' rights arguments, but he wanted the federal government to be guided by Congress and the courts rather than by a strong executive branch. His sympathies lay with the underdog and hence generally with the Democrats, yet he was too independent to go down the line with them. He deplored the party's addiction to William Jennings Bryan, whom he thought crazy on the silver issue and lacking in executive ability. The dark horse he and Cobb favored, with increasing ardor from 1906 on, was Woodrow Wilson. In New York politics, the *World* fought Tammany in season and out. Twice it helped elect that doughty Republican Charles Evans Hughes to the governorship, having pushed him into prominence in the first place as an investigator of the life-insurance company scandals it exposed in 1905. Toward the Republican Roosevelt, the paper was at times cordial, even enthusiastic. It hailed his trust busting, and was perhaps the first to nominate him for the Nobel peace prize for helping settle the Russo-Japanese War. Later, however, Pulitzer's conservative view of the Presidency was offended by what he considered T. R.'s jingoism, immodesty, and intemperate speech; J. P. flayed Roosevelt, in one of his many rapid-fire (and equally intemperate) talks with Cobb, as "a flamboyant, roughriderish, bullyboyish, cowhiding swashbuckler."

On most political issues, Cobb and Pulitzer saw eye to eye, but that left plenty of other subjects for combat. On April 10, 1907, his sixtieth birthday, Pulitzer resigned as president of his two publishing companies, in St. Louis and New York, in favor of his eldest son, Ralph. From his retreat on the Riviera he cabled a

Mr. Roosevelt is mistaken. He cannot muzzle **The World**. . . . *We repeat what we have already said—that the Congress of the United States should make a thorough investigation of the whole Panama transaction, that the full truth may be known to the American people. . . . This is the first time a President ever . . . proposed, in the absence of specific legislation, the criminal prosecution by the Government of citizens who criticised the conduct of the Government. . . . If* The World *has libelled anybody we hope it will be punished, but we do not intend to be intimidated by Mr. Roosevelt's threats, or by Mr. Roosevelt's denunciation, or by Mr. Roosevelt's power.*

December 16, 1908

farewell message which, while designed to be read at employees' dinners in the two cities, embodied a stirring statement of his philosophy of journalism and was clearly addressed to the world at large. He had polished it for days. In St. Louis, the *Post-Dispatch* printed it—and indeed continues to print it in capital letters under its masthead on the editorial page. In New York, other papers published the message, but not the *World*. Cobb would have none of it. J. P. had already resigned as editor of the *World* in another ringing statement back in 1890, early in his invalidism. One resignation was enough. Besides, Cobb knew better than anyone that Joseph Pulitzer could not for the life of him resign in any meaningful sense as long as he breathed. Why pretend? The blind man fairly howled with rage, but the deed was done. Cobb would run the message in his own way, and in his own good time.

Notwithstanding this episode, the climate abruptly improved. The following month J. P. sent word from Carlsbad that he had actually enjoyed the editorial

page of late, "and particularly enjoyed your brisk, vigorous letters." What in the world had come over him? The answer was delightfully simple. In writing Pulitzer the letters he demanded, Cobb had at last struck a tone that made his anguished employer laugh. One Cobb letter that month ran this way:

. . . Am devoting most of my energy to helping [Governor Charles Evans] Hughes, and nobody needs help more than he does. He is improving in many things, however. Coming down from Albany the other day he said to [Louis] Seibold [chief of the *World*'s Albany bureau]: "God damn that man Hearst." Then he repeated it three times. That's doing very well for a hard shell Baptist who has been superintendent of a Sunday School.

It is only less meritorious in its way than Roosevelt's remark to Tim Woodruff [a G.O.P. wheel-horse in New York] about Oswald Villard [publisher of the *Evening Post*]. Something was said about Villard and the *Evening Post*, and Woodruff asked Roosevelt if he knew Villard. T. R. snapped his jaws together and gurgled: "You will excuse my French, Woodruff, but he's a s-n-of-a-b-tch."

I believe this is all the village gossip there is this week.

Samples of Cobb's dry wit spiced life for the Chief as the two grew more closely attuned. Once Cobb scribbled, "This might interest Mr. Pulitzer" across the top of a letter from a reader, and sent it along; the letter began, "There is at least one thing for which your paper stands alone—its silly editorials. . . . You need an editorial writer, and badly, at that." When J. P. blistered Cobb for failing to read an editorial in the New York *Herald*, Cobb sent him a statement solemnly swearing that he had done so—attested by the *World*'s notary public. There was this gentle ribbing after a bet Cobb won: "By the way, I collected that Panama hat, which you told me to get, but . . . do you think an editorial writer can wear a hat like that, and retain his full measure of sympathy with the toiling Democratic masses?" And this, reflecting their avid interest in American history: "I am sending you Franklin Pierce's *Federal Usurpation* . . . God help him, he seems to be a Jeffersonian Democrat, which in this day is quite as ridiculous as being a mastodon." A Cobb epigram for J. P. on what we now call the Progressive Era: "There will soon be nothing left to reform except the weather." Cobb to Pulitzer on New York's Mayor George B. McClellan, Jr., son of the Civil War general: "He is the son of his father. Just as he starts to do something it rains, and he has to go back into camp again." Cobb on William Randolph Hearst during a mayoralty campaign: "We are trying to treat Hearst 'without prejudice,' as you say, but I confess it is a damned hard job so far as I am concerned. I *am* prejudiced against Hearst. . . . Some day I shall consider it a precious privilege if you will lift the lid and give me permission to scatter his intestines from the Battery to the Bronx."

A few years later, the subject of mayoral candidate William J. Gaynor, who was to succeed the drear McClellan, inspired these lines for Pulitzer's private delectation: "Our friend, the 'Christian jurist,' will probably be elected. He has done what he reasonably could do to defeat himself, but the time was too short. ... If he is really sane, I doubt if anyone was ever crazy; yet there is much to be said in favor of having

---

Lincoln once said that this Republic was founded on the rule of "root, hog, or die," and women are no less amenable to that principle than are men.... The woman who is sheltered today may be working in a factory tomorrow to support herself and her children. Hunger knows no sex. Want knows no sex. Necessity knows no sex. Property knows no sex. Only the ballot box knows sex.... In the steady sweep of democracy the time will come when the present opposition to woman suffrage will seem as short sighted and senseless as the former opposition to manhood suffrage now seems.

March 14, 1915

---

a lively lunatic at the head of the city government for four years. Nothing has been gained by a safe and sane administration; so it is possible that an energetic crazy man could do some good."

Part of their new-found rapport rested on Cobb's talent for poking fun both at himself and at his hypercritical mentor. "Seitz is away on vacation," he confided, "and I have nobody to quarrel with. That is very depressing.... I shall soon be 40 years old, and that is the most depressing thing of all. Forty is ten years older than 39, although I believe you hold to the theory that everybody is a damned fool until he is 40, and not necessarily very intelligent after that."

Wary of subordinates who got swelled heads, Pulitzer never bestowed on Cobb the title of editor of the *World*, which Merrill had worn. Criticism continued like a drum beat, issue after issue. Now, however, it was sprinkled with "my dear boy" (once he called Cobb "my adopted son," sending him, as he had to sons Ralph and Joseph, Lord Chesterfield's *Letters*), and his tone mellowed perceptibly: "And now forgive me and light a cigar and do read the news and pick out the right facts," or, "Forgive me dear boy, child, son, anything affectionate, but why call McClellan all these names? ... Is it consistent with your dignity as an unbiased judge?"

How much even these tempered admonitions would grate upon a man of Cobb's intellect and spirit may be surmised. Periodically he sent Pulitzer his resignation,

which J. P. simply ignored. In the end, the sulphurous old man's personal magnetism, courage in adversity, and total devotion to the paper and its causes—progressive causes like vigorous antitrust enforcement (Pulitzer wanted jail terms), lower tariffs, the direct election of senators, the adoption of a graduated federal income tax, and the elimination of campaign contributions by corporations, in all of which Cobb deeply believed—could not but hold his editor, head and heart, to the fire. J. P. ran a far more rigorous school of journalism than any of the formal ones his famous legacy to Columbia served to inspire, and the discipline he imposed, in Cobb's case almost always in the direction of restraint and fair-mindedness, unquestionably served to mold a greater editor.

Cobb even came to wear his scars proudly. "Four years ago today," he wrote Pulitzer on May 9, 1908, "I began work on the World. You will believe me, I know, when I say I would not barter these four years for any other years of my life." Pulitzer did believe him, for by now he knew his man. In December of that year, the two held a long skull session aboard J. P.'s new ocean-going hospital, the colossal steam yacht *Liberty*, off New York Harbor. Cobb's long memorandum of the conversation shows the forever dissatisfied one insisting that "the news treatment of politics and allied subjects must be raised, in temper, tone, accuracy, restraint, and moral courage, to the level ... [of] the editorial columns." Accordingly, Pulitzer outlined an experimental plan to make Cobb his overseer of both the news and editorial departments, "to the end that Mr. P.'s principles of journalism shall be ... indelibly stamped upon the news columns ... and that if possible the Pulitzer tradition shall remain with the *World* long after Mr. Pulitzer and also Mr. Cobb are dead." The scheme never quite materialized, but it suggests the publisher's esteem for Cobb. "The Page" was enough for Cobb. "You once said that there was more joy in making an editorial page than in anything else you knew of," he wrote Pulitzer in 1910. "I fully agree with you."

Not that editor and publisher had achieved permanent sweetness and light. They did enter a solemn compact, according to Seitz, "not to get mad at each other at the same time." It went for naught. After a furious dispute aboard the *Liberty* once, Pulitzer ordered Cobb put off at Atlantic Highlands, New Jersey, well after dark. The captain of the ship pointed out that there was no transportation to New York at that hour. Pulitzer shot back that his orders were to be obeyed, a boat was lowered, and Cobb was duly deposited on the lonely shore. (How he got home that night the records leave us to imagine.) Ralph Pulitzer's dutifully recorded memorandum of another set-to aboard the

Liberty shows that his father bridled when Cobb spoke of another editorial writer as helpful because he knew Mr. P.'s mind. No one knew his mind, snapped Pulitzer. If that were the case, Cobb retorted dryly, then Frank I. Cobb ought to be drowned.

Reflecting Pulitzer's insistence that the editorial page stay abreast of the day's news—he would throw a tantrum or accuse his editors of deliberately torturing him if the paper failed to comment on a major news development, no matter how late the news broke—Cobb worked incontinently long hours. Reading, researching, interviewing, briskly testing ideas and phrases on others in the corridors, in the city room, in the *World's* restaurant, keeping a hawk's eye on all the other papers as he shaped his leader, he would turn to it only at the eleventh hour, locking himself in his small room in the dome and battering his typewriter in pent-up fury. His first marriage having ended in divorce, he gave up his home in Staten Island in 1909 and moved into a West Side flat, the better to follow this regimen, and though for years he smouldered over the injustice of the long hours, he finally admitted to Ralph Pulitzer that J. P. was right: the *World* was completely *au courant,* and there was nothing like it anywhere.

At length, Cobb appeared to be buckling under the strain. "Take entire week off for needed rest," J. P. cabled in the spring of 1911. Two days later Pulitzer forgetfully cabled him fresh instructions ("more short, talk-making editorials for Sunday page") and questions for immediate response. But that summer, Pulitzer gave his editor a six-week vacation in Europe, a trip that Cobb, by this time drawing a lordly $250 a week, could easily have afforded himself. J. P. not only paid his way, but took pains to instruct the captain and chief steward of the *Baltic* to look after him. (When J. P. gave an order, the whole White Star line snapped to attention, because for years he had been the firm's most prodigal customer.) Cobb dutifully sat at the captain's table and was all but suffocated with service. This and weeks of lazing in the English countryside restored him.

Pulitzer greeted Cobb's first efforts upon his return with glee. Buy a hundred first-class cigars on me, he wrote, "but don't . . . smoke more than three daily for your health." Cobb bristled at such largess at times, but he did get the cigars—"I'm smoking *two* a day, thus showing my power of self-restraint." There were still a few left, at that rate, when word came from the *Liberty* in Charleston Harbor that Joseph Pulitzer was dead.

Writing the *World's* valedictory to its publisher on October 30, 1911, Cobb remembered the message he had spiked four years earlier. ". . . Mr. Pulitzer's idea of a great newspaper was concisely expressed in a cablegram . . . on the occasion of his sixtieth birthday—

An institution which should always fight for progress and reform; never tolerate injustice or corruption; always fight demagogues of all parties; never belong to any party; always oppose privileged classes and public plunder; never lack sympathy with the poor; always remain devoted to the public welfare; never be satisfied with merely printing the news; always be drastically independent; never be afraid to attack wrong, whether by predatory plutocracy or predatory poverty."

Except in the *Post-Dispatch's* circulation area, where J. P.'s words sound as brave and as pertinent as they did in 1907, there is a ring of pathos in them because "always," in the case of the *World,* turned out to be less than twenty years after Pulitzer's death. (The Scripps-Howard people bought what was left of it in February, 1931.) But there was never anything pathetic about them to Cobb. Editor of the *World* at last, he held the paper to its creed for the rest of his tragically brief life. No editor in the land more effectively championed Woodrow Wilson's "New Freedom" before the First World War, nor his course during that war, nor the League of Nations after it. Cobb remembered, too, Pulitzer's prophetic admonition less than two months before he died: "Be kind and gentle with Woodrow Wilson, but when he goes astray, lead him back." No one criticized Wilson more discerningly, on the very points most historians do today—the too-partisan call for a Democratic Congress in 1918, the failure to include notable Republicans like William Howard Taft and Elihu Root on the peace commission, his toleration of Jim Crowism in government departments (for which Cobb blistered him to some effect), and the sad delusion that he might run again in 1920.

Perhaps O. K. Bovard, the celebrated managing editor of the *Post-Dispatch,* who was another battle-hardened graduate of Pulitzer's personal school of journalism, had it right. The light really went out of the *World,* Bovard noted privately years later, on December 21, 1923—the day Frank Cobb died of cancer. In his own way, Cobb deserves the eulogy he gave Woodrow Wilson at the conclusion of the moving editorial that filled the whole page of the *World* on Wilson's last day in office. They are the words of Paul the Apostle to Timothy:

"I have fought a good fight, I have finished my course, I have kept the faith."

Mr. Starr is the director of both the Oral History Research Office at Columbia University and the International Division of the School of Journalism there. His article is based in large part on the Pulitzer Papers at Columbia.

For further reading: Pulitzer, by W. A. Swanberg (Scribner, 1967); Cobb of the World: A Leader in Liberalism, *Cobb editorials compiled by John L. Heaton (Dutton, 1924).*

packet bound for New Orleans. A heat wave was his undoing; discovery of the decomposing corpse led to his arrest. Sam went to John's defense, engaging Cousin Dudley and Robert Emmet as attorneys and scrounging about for funds.

The trial was the newspaper sensation of the year, for it had all the elements of melodrama: a crime of passion, a voluble defendant with friends of influence and means, an aroused populace, a lovely black-eyed blonde, and a bizarre climax.

The girl in the story was Caroline Henshaw, an unschooled young woman who gave birth to a son just before the trial opened in January of 1842. She told the court that she had met John Colt in Philadelphia in 1840, but did not live with him until she came to New York the following January. He taught her to read and write, but eschewed marriage, he said, because of his poverty. Another version had it that Caroline was of German birth, and that it was Sam, not John, who met her first. On his trip to Europe in 1835, the story went, Sam met Caroline in Scotland and brought her back to America as his wife. According to this account, Sam was so preoccupied with his inventions and was away so much that John had, out of pity, made Caroline his common-law wife. Furthermore, because of their social differences, Sam was only too glad to be rid of a partner who might impede his career, which he always placed above personal ties.

In any event, John Colt was convicted of murdering Sam Adams and was sentenced to be hanged on November 18, 1842.

As dawn broke that day, Sam Colt was the first to see John. At about eleven o'clock, Dr. Henry Anthon, rector of St. Mark's Church, visited the prisoner, who had decided, after conferring with his brother, to make Caroline his lawful wife. John handed the minister five hundred dollars to be used for Caroline's welfare; he had received the money from Sam—a sizable gift from a man whose factory had failed the month before. A little before noon, Caroline, worn and nervous but smartly dressed in a claret-colored coat and carrying a muff, arrived with Sam. She and John were married by Dr. Anthon. For nearly an hour she remained alone with John in his cell. Then she departed with Sam, and John was left undisturbed.

At five minutes to four the sheriff and Dr. Anthon entered the cell to escort John to the scaffold. But the prisoner lay dead on his bed, a knife with a broken handle buried in his heart. The New York *Herald*

speculated that Colt's relatives knew of his intention to commit suicide and that they might have smuggled the knife into his cell. The allegation was never proved —or disproved.

Colt secretly arranged for Caroline and her young son to go to Germany. He told his brother James that she "speaks and understands German and can best be cared for in the German countries. . . . [I have] made all the necessary arrangements and will somehow provide the needful." At his insistence she changed her name to Miss Julia Leicester, but the boy grew up as Samuel Caldwell Colt.

Caroline and her son remained abroad, supported by Sam. Eventually she became attracted to a young Prussian officer, Baron Friedrich Von Oppen, whose father questioned her background and suspected that money, not love, was Caroline's motive. But Colt used all his influence to insure a quiet marriage and afterward did everything possible to make the couple and fifteen-year-old Samuel happy.

Apparently the boy did not like book learning any better than Sam himself, so Colt brought him back to America and placed him in a private school. He loaned Caroline $1,000 to enable her husband, who had been disinherited, to enter business. The money was soon dissipated, and Caroline feared debtor's prison. Sam came to the rescue again, making the Baron his agent in Belgium. But Von Oppen and Caroline drifted apart, and she was lonely without her child. She appealed to Sam to bring her back to America—and there the curtain drops: the beautiful, tormented Caroline Henshaw Colt Von Oppen vanished from Samuel Colt's life just as he reached the pinnacle of success. She never appeared again, except in a portrait that hung beside one of John Colt at Armsmear, and in the persistent stories (Hartford residents have never let them die) about her true relationship to Samuel Colt.

Even before the demise of the Paterson company in 1842, Colt had been working on two other inventions. In the late thirties he began developing a waterproof cartridge out of tin foil, and he also returned to his experiments with underwater batteries. About the latter he wrote to President John Tyler in 1841:

Discoveries since Fulton's time combined with an invention original with myself, enable me to effect instant destruction of either Ships or Steamers . . . on their entering a harbour.

The Navy granted him $6,000 for a test. Using copper wire insulated with layers of waxed and tarred twine, he made four successful demonstrations, one of which blew up a sixty-ton schooner on the Potomac before a host of congressmen. But neither the military nor Congress took to the idea, which John Quincy Adams branded an "unChristian contraption," and Colt's Submarine Battery Company never surfaced.

The waterproof cartridges had a better reception, including an endorsement by Winfield Scott, General in Chief of the Army. In 1845 Congress spent one quarter of its $200,000 state militia appropriation on Colt's ammunition.

Meanwhile, Colt had become acquainted with Professor Samuel F. B. Morse and his electro-magnetic telegraph. The two inventors hit it off from the start. If Colt's cable could carry an electrical impulse under water to trigger an explosive charge, then it probably could carry telegraphic messages across lakes and rivers. Colt supplied Morse with batteries and wire and won a contract for laying forty miles of wire from Washington to Baltimore. In May of 1846, the same month in which war was declared on Mexico, the New York and Offing Magnetic Telegraph Association was incorpo-

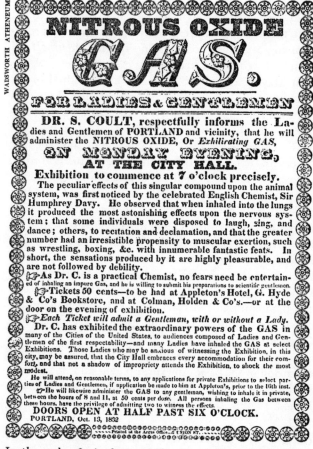

In the early 1830's the would-be arms maker, struggling to make ends meet, was billing himself as the "celebrated Dr. Coult"—purveyor of laughing gas at fifty cents a whiff.

rated by Colt and a new set of investors, with the rights to construct a telegraph line from New York City to Long Island and New Jersey. But again the operation was mismanaged, partly because of Colt's negligence, and at thirty-two he once more found himself as "poor as a churchmouse." Desperate, he sought—in vain—a captaincy in a new rifle regiment.

Although Colt was not destined to fight in the Mexican War, his guns were. For the five-shot Paterson pistol, having won acceptance against the Seminoles in Florida, had gained further renown in the hands of the Texas Rangers in the early forties. (The six-shot Colt .45, or "Peacemaker," the gun that supposedly won the West, did not appear until the early 1870's.) In the summer of 1844, for instance, Captain John C. Hays and fifteen rangers engaged some eighty Comanches in open combat along the Pedernales River and with Colt guns killed or wounded half of them. Altogether, 2,700 Paterson guns, mostly .34 and .36 caliber, were made for the frontiersmen in pocket, belt, and holster sizes. At the close of 1846, without money or machines but still possessed of his patent rights, Colt approached Ranger Captain Samuel H. Walker about buying "improved" arms for his men, who had been mustered into the United States Army. A veteran Indian fighter, Walker needed little encouragement. He wrote Colt:

Without your pistols we would not have had the confidence to have undertaken such daring adventures. . . . With improvements I think they can be rendered the most perfect weapon in the World for light mounted troops. . . . The people throughout Texas are anxious to procure your pistols.

That was certainly the case with General Zachary Taylor, commanding troops in Texas in the autumn of 1846. Taylor wanted one thousand Colts within three months, but Colt lacked even a model with which to start manufacturing again. That did not overly distress Colt, because Captain Walker wanted a simpler yet heavier gun—.44 caliber—that would fire six shots. So Colt designed the so-called Walker gun.

Armed with a $25,000 government order, Sam persuaded Eli Whitney, Jr., the Connecticut contractor for Army muskets, to make the thousand revolvers. They were ready six months later. A pair of guns for Walker, who had hounded Colt for delivery, arrived in Mexico only four days before he was killed in action. To General Sam Houston, who had praised the guns' superiority, Colt wrote:

I am truly pleased to lern . . . that your influance unasked for by a poor devil of an inventor has from your own sense of right been employed to du away the prejudice heretofore existing among men who have the power to promote or crush at pleasure all improvements in Fire arms for military purposes.

His appetite whetted, Colt obtained an order for another thousand Walker guns. He borrowed about $5,000 from his banker cousin Elisha Colt and other Hartford businessmen, leased a factory on Pearl Street, and hired scores of hands. Thus, in the summer of 1847, Colt started his own factory, promising to turn out five thousand guns a year. To a friend in Illinois he wrote a letter that reveals much of the basic Colt:

I am working on my own hook and have sole control and management of my business and intend to keep it as long as I live without being subject to the whims of a pack of dam fools and knaves styling themselves a board of directors ... my arms sustain a high reputation among men of brains in Mexico and ... now is the time to make money out of them.

Alert to the new methods being used in New England's machine-tool industry, Colt quickly adapted the system of interchangeable parts to the mass production of guns. Though two other Connecticut gunmakers, Simeon North and Whitney, had been the first to standardize parts, Colt perfected the technique to the point where eighty per cent of his gunmaking was done by machine alone.

Vital to his success was his able staff, especially Elisha Root, whom he had first met at Ware and whom he had now lured away from the Collins Axe Company by offering him the unheard-of salary of $5,000 a year. As Colt's head superintendent, Root designed and constructed the incomparable Colt armory and installed its equipment. During his tenure, Root invented many ingenious belt-driven machines (some of which are still operative) for turning gun stocks, boring and rifling barrels, and making cartridges.

Root's quiet, firm, perfectionist leadership made Colt's factory a training center for a succession of gifted mechanics, some of whom went on to apply his modern methods in their own companies. Charles E. Billings and Christopher M. Spencer started a company (now defunct) for making a variety of hand tools; Spencer invented the Spencer rifle, used in the Civil War, as well as the first screw-making machine. Other armory graduates included Francis A. Pratt and Amos Whitney, who together founded a machine-tool company that today is part of Colt Industries.

While Root managed the factory, Colt functioned as president and salesman extraordinary. Far more than his competitors, he appreciated the necessity of creating demand through aggressive promotion. He paid military officers and others to act as his agents in the West and the South and as his lobbyists in Congress, while Colt himself solicited patronage from state governors. Until the approach of the Civil War, however, government sales were scanty compared to the thousands of revolvers shipped to California during the Gold Rush, or to foreign heads of state. From 1849 on, Colt travelled abroad extensively, wangling introductions to government officials and making them gifts of beautifully engraved weapons.

In May of 1851 Colt exhibited five hundred of his machine-made guns and served free brandy at London's Crystal Palace Exposition. He even read a paper, "Rotating Chambered-Breech Firearms," to the Institute of Civil Engineers. Two years later he became the first American manufacturer to open a branch abroad, choosing a location on the Thames for supplying the English government with what he termed "the best peesmakers" in the world. So backward did he find England's mechanical competence, however, that he was forced to send over both journeymen and machines. Colt was ultimately unable to convince the English of the superiority of machine labor, and the London factory was sold in 1857, but not before it and the main plant in Hartford had between them supplied two hundred thousand pistols for use in the Crimean War.

Colt had been successful in obtaining a seven-year extension of his basic American patent and in crushing attempts at infringement. He had become a millionaire in less than a decade. As a loyal Democrat he had

On prominent display at New York City's Crystal Palace in 1853, Colt's weapons were extolled in the press for their "safety, simplicity, durability, accuracy and celerity of fire, force of penetration, and security against moisture."

finally won his long-sought commission, becoming a colonel and aide-de-camp to his good friend Governor Thomas Seymour.

As demand and production continued to soar, Colt had to seek larger quarters. By the early fifties his dream was to build the largest private armory anywhere. He turned his attention to two hundred acres of lowlands along the Connecticut River below Hartford, which he planned to reclaim by building a dike nearly two miles long against spring flooding. His dike, with French osiers planted on top to prevent erosion, was finished in two years at a cost of $125,000.

Behind the dike soon rose the brownstone armory, with a blue onion-shaped dome topped by a gold ball and a stallion holding a broken spear in its mouth. A giant 250-horsepower steam engine, its flywheel thirty feet in diameter, drove four hundred various machines by a labyrinth of shafts and belts. By 1857 Colt was turning out 250 finished guns a day.

The buildings were steam heated and gas lighted. Around them he constructed fifty multiple dwellings, in rows, for his workmen and their families; he had streets laid out and a reservoir built. Colt paid good wages but insisted on maximum effort in return. Said one factory notice, evidently written by Colt himself:
EVERY MAN EMPLOYED IN OR ABOUT MY ARMOURY WHETHER BY PIECEWIRK OR BY DAYS WIRK IS EXPECTED TO WIRK TEN HOURS DURING THE RUNING OF THE ENGINE, & NO ONE WHO DOSE NOT CHEARFULLY CONCENT TO DU THIS NEED EXPECT TO BE EMPLOYED BY ME.

By "inside contracting" Colt kept his own employment rolls to less than a fourth of the total number who earned their living from the armory. His thirty-one contractors assumed responsibility for their particular operations or departments, hiring their own men and receiving materials and tools from Colt.

The willow trees grew so well on top of the dike that Colt set up a small factory to manufacture willow furniture, which became especially popular in Cuba and South America because of its lightness of weight and its coolness. For his German willow workers he erected a row of two-family brick houses modelled after their homes in Potsdam, and gave them a beer-and-coffee garden as well. For his own pleasure and theirs, he formed them into a brightly uniformed armory band. His final, most forward-looking contribution to his employees' welfare was Charter Oak Hall, named after the Charter Oak tree that fell in 1856, the year the hall was dedicated.* Seating a thousand

* The Charter Oak long had been a symbol of Connecticut's passion for independence. In 1687 the British royal governor was frustrated in his attempt to take away the colony's charter when a local resident stashed the document in the ancient tree.

people, the hall was a meeting place for workers; there they could read, hear lectures or concerts, and hold fairs or dances.

Through it all, Sam Colt had remained a rather bibulous bachelor, a well-fleshed six-footer whose light hazel eyes were beginning to gather more than a few wrinkles about them. But Colonel Colt was now at the peak of his career, and he needed a wife and home; these he acquired with his usual dispatch and pomp. Four years earlier he had met the two daughters of the Reverend William Jarvis of Middletown, downriver from Hartford. He chose as his bride the gracious and gentle Elizabeth, who at thirty was twelve years younger than he. The extravagance of their wedding, on June 5, 1856, rocked Hartford's staid society. The steamboat *Washington Irving*, which Colt chartered for the occasion, carried him and his friends to the wedding in Middletown. They boarded in front of the flag-bedecked armory; there was an immense crowd of spectators, and Colt mechanics fired a rifle salute from the cupola. Two days later the Colonel and his bride sailed on the *Baltic* for a six-month trip to Europe. On their return, Sam began to build his palatial Armsmear on the western edge of his property.

When Armsmear was finished, Colt's investment in the South Meadows was close to two million dollars—truly a gigantic redevelopment project for that era (and one that he accomplished without borrowing from the bankers he so roundly detested). Yet its importance was largely lost upon the city fathers, and Colt's father-in-law complained, "Though he pays nearly one tenth of the whole city tax, yet there has been a determination on the part of the Republicans to do nothing for him, or the many hundreds who reside on his property in the South Meadows."

Although the city finally gave him some tax relief for his improvements, its only physical contribution was three street lamps. And when Sam started a private ferry from the armory across the Connecticut to East Hartford to convey mechanics who could not be accommodated in company housing, the hostile Hartford *Courant* accused him of trying to "dodge the rights of the Hartford Bridge Company." So exasperated did the Colonel become over such treatment—which was undoubtedly aggravated by his own brashness—that he made a major change in his will, depriving Connecticut of what would surely have been a great educational institution. He had originally planned to leave a quarter of his estate for "founding a school for the education of practical mechanics and engineers."

By the end of 1858 the Colonel, his lady, and young Caldwell were comfortably ensconced in Armsmear. The family saw little of Colt, however; as the North and South raced toward cataclysm, Colt was busy making enormous profits by filling the demands of both sides for what he sardonically called "my latest work on 'Moral Reform.' " He seriously considered building a branch armory in either Virginia or Georgia. The Armory's earnings averaged $237,000 annually until the outbreak of the Civil War, when they soared to over a million. His last shipment of five hundred guns to the South left for Richmond three days after Fort Sumter, packed in boxes marked "hardware."

Colt regarded slavery not as a moral wrong but as an inefficient economic system. He abhorred abolitionists, denounced John Brown as a traitor, and opposed the election of Lincoln for fear the Union would be destroyed—and a lucrative market thereby lost. Like many other Connecticut manufacturers, he believed that an upset of the status quo would be ruinous to the free trade on which the state's prosperity depended. Thus, he took a conservative stand on slavery and supported the Democrats because they stressed Union and the Constitution. But at the same time, he shrewdly prepared the armory for a five-year conflict and for the arming of a million men; the prevailing sentiment in Hartford was that a civil war, if it broke out, could not last two months. During a vacation in Cuba in early 1861, Colt wrote Root and Lord, exhorting them to "run the Armory night & day with a double set of hands. . . . Make hay while the sun shines."

During the 1860 state elections Colt's political convictions and their manifestations caused a stir in the press, the *Courant* leading the attack and the Hartford *Times* waging a vigorous defense. Colt was known to have used dubious methods in previous campaigns, including having ballot boxes watched to make sure his workers supported Democratic candidates. This time the hostile press accused him of discharging, outright, "66 men, of whom 56 are Republicans. . . . Many of these were contractors and among his oldest and ablest workmen." Asserting that their dismissals amounted to "proscription for political opinion," the discharged Republican workers resolved that "the oppression of free labor by capital, and the attempt to coerce and control the votes of free men, is an outrage upon the rights of the laboring classes." Colt quickly issued a flat denial:

In no case have I ever hired an operative or discharged one for his political or religious opinions. I hire them for ten hours labor . . . and for that I pay them punctually every month. . . .

Yet a few months earlier he had suggested to a politician friend that he pen a resolution urging "us [manufacturers] all to discharge from our imploymen every Black Republican . . . until the question of slavery is for ever set to rest & the rights of the South secured permanently to them."

Now Colt's immense business responsibilities were beginning to wear down his seemingly inexhaustible energies. Bothered by frequent attacks of inflammatory rheumatism and distressed by the death of an infant daughter, he drove himself as if he knew his days were numbered. Smoking Cuban cigars, Colt ruled his domain from a roll-top desk at the armory, often writing his own letters in his left-handed scrawl.

Shortly before he died, he handed the family reins to his brother-in-law, Richard Jarvis, with the admonition that "you and your family must do for me now as I have no one else to call upon. You are the pendulum that must keep the works in motion." Two of his own brothers were dead, and the other, James, a hot-tempered ne'er-do-well and petty politician, had proved a miserable failure as Colt's manager in the short-lived London plant and later as an official of the armory. The entire estate, which Mrs. Colt and their son Caldwell controlled, was valued at $15,000,000—an enormous sum in those days—giving Elizabeth an income of $200,000 a year for life. Caldwell grew up to be a good sportsman, an international yachtsman, and a lover of beautiful women; although a vice president, he took little interest in the company, and died a mysterious death in Florida at the age of thirty-six.

Other than Elizabeth and Caldwell, Colt's major beneficiary was Master Samuel Caldwell Colt, "son of my late brother John Caldwell Colt," whom even Mrs. Colt regarded favorably. When Sam and his southern bride were married in a large and fashionable wedding at Armsmear in 1863, Elizabeth presented the couple with a house across the street; at her death she left them many of her personal effects. For a short time this handsome, retiring man worked at the armory; he became a director but eventually moved to Farmington and took up gentleman farming. He was always loyal to the memory of Colonel Colt, who his descendants believe was his true father.

Colonel Samuel Colt had adopted as his motto *Vincit qui patitur*, "He conquers who suffers." But a better-fitting key to his character is found in a remark he once wrote to his half-brother William: " 'It is better to be at the head of a louse than at the tail of a lyon!' . . . If I cant be first I wont be second in anything."

Colt's ambition was to be first and best, and his means were money and power, both of which he had in full measure. His patriotism, while stronger than that of the average munitions maker, was ever subordinate to his desire to see maintained a commercially favorable status quo between North and South. Colt was not above using bribery and was unashamed of profiteering; he seldom reflected on the moral implications of dealing in weapons of death and destruction.

In fairness, Colt was not alone in his evident amorality: the turbulence of the age had thrown out of focus more than a few of the old values for more than a few of his countrymen. Especially to Connecticut Yankees, who had made their state an arsenal for the nation since colonial days, gunmaking could be no sin. What did bother the diluted Puritan conscience of Colt's time was that a Hartford aristocrat flouted the tenets of the Congregational Church to which he was born— by a bizarre career, a love of high living, and an overbearing pride and flamboyance.

It can scarcely be denied that Sam Colt was one of America's first tycoons, a Yankee peddler who became a dazzling entrepreneur. The success of his many mechanical inventions and refinements was due less to their intrinsic merits—which were considerable—than to his showmanship in telling the world about them. He achieved his goals despite continual adversity for nearly three fourths of his short life. Proud, stubborn, and farsighted, he was a man apart; he was impatient with the old ways, preferring, as he said, to be "paddling his own canoe."

A resident of Hartford, Mr. Grant contributed an article on the Connecticut River to our April, 1967, issue. One of the best sources for his study of Sam Colt was William B. Edwards' Story of Colt's Revolvers *(Stackpole, 1953).*

The Purple Mountains' Fading Majesty

CONTINUED FROM PAGE 47

work, building modern little mills to take advantage of newly developed techniques for removing metal from refractory chemical combinations. Relief agencies even conducted classes in gold panning, and here and there, during summers, one saw families camped beside streams while the husbands sought to eke out a dollar or two a day washing gravel as it had been washed seventy-five years earlier by the first stampeders.

It was no true revival, however. The bonanza ores were gone, and the essential smallness of the operations was underscored by the giant bones among which they pawed. Still, such operations provided a living for a few people—until the Second World War. Instantly the gold mines were denied priorities for materials. Shortages closed them down—soaring costs would soon have had the same effect, anyway—and eight decades of often overblown romance, wherein the tail seemed frequently to be wagging the dog, came to an end.

Mining, of course, did not stop; emphasis merely shifted—to the copper of Butte, Montana, and Bingham Canyon, Utah; to the lead that accompanied the silver of the Coeur d'Alene in Idaho; to zinc in the narrow canyon of the Eagle River below Colorado's Tennessee Pass; to molybdenum at Climax, high above Leadville; and, very mysteriously at the time, to the carnotite ores pocketed in the plateau country bordering the San Miguel River a few dozen miles below Telluride. Carnotite yields both vanadium oxide (red cake) and uranium oxide (yellow cake). When the carnotite mines reopened late in the thirties we assumed that the goal was vanadium oxide, to be used in hardening steel. We were wrong. Under impenetrable secrecy, yellow cake began moving to an ultramodern research complex at a place called Los Alamos in the Jemez Mountains north of Santa Fe. Years later, when the bomb went off at Hiroshima, we knew.

War-born improvements in technology turned the surviving metal mines into giants. By the mid-1960's Bingham Canyon, Utah, was turning out upwards of 80,000 tons of copper ore *each day*—more ore per twenty-four hours than the narrow-gauge railroad had hauled away from Red Mountain in four full years!

In fact, so far as annual tonnages were concerned, mining was back. It did not seem like the old days, however. The new effort was concentrated, leaving hundreds of once-active claims untouched, their tunnels and cabins slowly collapsing. The serpentine supply trains of livestock, their cavernous barns and profane herders, and the ranchers who once had grown fodder for the animals all vanished. The little railroads disappeared. Automation eased the gruelling labor inside the earth; at a new molybdenum mine, opened in 1967 in Clear Creek Canyon, Colorado, a single worker can tell by a glance at a television screen which ore bin far underground needs filling, an operation he then completes by pushing a button. The 4,000 or more inhabitants that Telluride's strenuous demands had once drawn to the town had shrunk by 1967 to fewer than 600. Burdened with an outmoded tax structure, the decrepit town faced, as most of the reduced mountain communities did, harrowing problems in maintaining schools, hospitals, sewage disposal plants, and other municipal services. That's what old-timers meant when they said that mining had not revived, whatever the tonnage figures proclaimed.

The drift of people away from the high country was more than counteracted by the rapid growth of cities near the foothills. Most of the newcomers who settled in these cities responded enthusiastically to the dry climate and the dramatic landscapes. College professors, according to one wry bit of folklore at the University of Colorado, were even expected to receive part of their salaries in sunshine, scenery, and pleasantly informal styles of living. Indigenous folk celebrations —rodeos, Indian dances, Spanish fiestas—caught the fancy of many of the new settlers. In New Mexico the architecture of the Pueblo Indians, as modified by the Spanish-Americans, completely won over the home builders settling around the new atomic plants. And only an hour from every major center—from Great Falls, Montana, to Albuquerque, New Mexico—lay the enthralling playgrounds of the national forests.

The salubrious climate and vigorous sports of the mountains had long been advertised, of course. Big-game hunters were attaching themselves to fur-trade caravans as early as the 1830's. In 1873, Denver's Committee of Asthmatics had printed one hundred case histories in pamphlet form and broadcast the hope of relief to sufferers throughout the nation. During the 1860's, dwellers in the high basins learned to travel about on long Norwegian skis, balancing themselves

with a single pole held slantwise in front of them; a few unconventional souls, banding into outing clubs, even used the devices for sport. Railroads eagerly promoted mineral-water spas where guests at ornate resort hotels amused themselves between sips by taking scenic drives in elegant coaches.

These things were exceptions, however. Until the advent of the automobile, outdoor recreation was limited to a few places and to relatively few people. Then, liberated by the new mobility that developed after World War I, venturesome families began visiting the Rockies in their own cars rather than aboard trains. At first most of the visitors sought out the national parks. Later, in the 1930's, increasing num-

bers took to bumping over the new fire and supply roads that the Civilian Conservation Corps was building deep into forests, where once only unmapped trails had led.

The surge was not limited to summer campers and autumn deer hunters. Stimulated by the success of the 1932 Winter Olympics at Lake Placid, New York, skiers began prowling the Rockies, looking for runs comparable to those in Switzerland. Hoping to fill empty train seats, officials of the Union Pacific hired a Swiss expert to locate a site to meet the demand. The spot finally selected was the old town of Ketchum on the Wood River of southern Idaho, once a lively center for the distribution of mining supplies and for the shipment of sheep to market. Turning up an eastern fork of the Wood River, the promoters built Sun Valley, first of the major Rocky Mountain ski resorts. The Denver & Rio Grande meanwhile promoted more modest sites in Colorado within reach of Denver and Boulder—Winter Park at the western portal of the Moffat Tunnel; the long hills near Hot Sulphur Springs in Middle Park, where William Byers had tried seventy years earlier to develop a summer resort; and Steamboat Springs on the Yampa River, where eventually some of the first American ski-jump records were established. Other weekend enthusiasts drove automobiles to the top of Berthoud Pass on U.S. Highway 40, then skied down swaths cut through the forest for telephone lines, and were picked up at the bottom of the improvised runs by friends who had volunteered to bring down the cars. Lifts? You were lucky, in those years, to find even a rope tow.

World War II slowed the stampede of recreationists. Afterward, the Depression gone, the number swelled even more prodigiously. Between 1946 and 1964, visits to the national forests in Colorado increased from 1,500,000 to 14,567,000 a year; in New Mexico, from 500,000 to 5,769,000; in Montana, from fewer than 1,000,000 to more than 7,000,000. And these enormous figures do not even include visitors to the national parks, monuments, or historic sites. Each fall, more than half a million Nimrods fanned out through the hills and harvested surprising amounts of wild meat —in 1964 an estimated 81,000 deer and 11,000 elk in Colorado alone.

In the winter the skiers came, seeking multimillion-dollar lifts that would enable them to plunge down as many miles in a weekend as some average prewar skiers had covered in a winter. To entertain and house these new enthusiasts, old towns were refurbished— Aspen in Colorado and Alta in Utah are two of the better-known ones. New towns also appeared—for instance, the carefully planned Tyrolean-style village of Vail, Colorado.

Motels, restaurants, garages, filling stations, outfitters, and storekeepers in existing towns were staggered by the concentrated demands of these fluid hordes. For a single example: the permanent population of Lake City, Colorado, located in the heart of a popular trout-fishing and deer-hunting area, is fewer than a hundred people. Then in July and August and for a while in October, upwards of a thousand restless transients flow through the town each day, expecting food, beds, gasoline, and miscellaneous supplies. Since local facilities in Lake City and a dozen towns like it can service only a small portion of the demand, a new kind of supplier has appeared: the man and his wife who during winter operate a desert dude ranch or motel or store in, say, Scottsdale, Arizona, and who at the beginning of the summer load their trucks with saddle horses and dude wranglers, with stocks of gay western clothing, with brooms and portable television sets, and head for the high country—modern-day Yankee peddlers.

Even the decrepit, forty-five-mile-long narrow-gauge railroad running from Durango, Colorado, up the awesome Animas Canyon to Silverton felt the shock. Tourists discovered the exotic little curiosity in the early 1950's, just when the D. & R.G.W. was preparing, with a sigh of relief, to shed the profitless spur. Such a clamor against abandonment arose that the railroad reconsidered. By 1967 two ramshackle strings of yellow observation cars were being hauled up the wavering tracks each summer day; the so-called Train to Yesterday had become one of the most popular tourist items in the Rocky Mountain area.

Towns overwhelmed by these jostling crowds were not quite sure how to shape their new identities. Some, like Montana's Virginia City, grew resolutely picturesque and reconstructed themselves to look, they hoped, as they had during the days of the Gold Rush. Others, like Colorado's Central City and Silverton, succumbed to the carnival trade and filled themselves with tawdry curio shops competing for attention by means of flamboyant signs and amplified barkers. Still others contented themselves with offering comfortable if somewhat standardized accommodations and varying entertainments. A favorite form of the latter was drama, ranging from serious experimental plays at places like Helena to old-time melodramas at Cripple Creek, Durango, and Jackson Hole. Critics of the scene are inclined to sneer at all of them—Samesville, U.S.A., Rocky Mountain style.

Inevitably a few of the people who rolled through the hills began to desire something more permanent than a motel room. Those with modest means obtained title to abandoned houses in the old mining

towns by paying the back taxes, then rebuilt the dwellings. More affluent visitors, especially skiers, began erecting second homes at Sun Valley, at Jackson Hole, at Aspen, and at half a dozen other spots. Summer cabins dotted the eastern flanks of the Big Horn Mountains, the meadows of Montana's Bitterroot Valley, the mesas back of Santa Fe. A surprising cultural drift accompanied this movement into mountain camps once notable for their crudeness. Ouray, Colorado, sought to emulate Taos, New Mexico, as an artist's colony; Central City produced lavish operas each summer; Aspen launched music festivals and intellectual seminars almost as rarefied as the mountain air. Towns as isolated as Cody and Big Horn in Wyoming and Helena in Montana built handsome museums to glorify the work of such western artists as Charles M. Russell and Frederic Remington.

Difficult though the problems of adjustment have been for the mountain hamlets, the strain placed on the national forests by recreationists has been even greater. For one thing, the towns wanted the new rush; the Forest Service, a branch of the Department of Agriculture originally devoted mainly to conservation, did not. Partly for that reason, the national forests were not nearly as well prepared for the rush as the Department of the Interior's National Park Service.

The Forest Service was work-oriented. A notion clung in the Rockies, and in much of America, that there was something faintly reprehensible about grown men playing around in the outdoors like unemployed Boy Scouts—unless they were hunting food, in the tradition of the pioneer providers. Thus it was culturally acceptable for rangers to join state fish and game departments in propagating wildlife, but otherwise their concerns were determinedly utilitarian.

Accustomed as they were to that kind of rationale, local supervisors at first looked sourly on the influx of recreationists brought by automobiles. During the early 1930's, they complained bitterly in their reports about taking care of people rather than forests—of hauling garbage, erecting directional signs, hunting for lost children, and answering foolish questions. Not until skiers began risking their lives en masse did a major shift in attitude occur.

To most dwellers in the high country, these new winter sportsmen were incomprehensible. We who lived there were afraid of snow. The toll of disasters

over two thirds of a century had been appalling. In 1874 an avalanche at Alta, Utah, killed more than sixty residents; the exact number was never determined. Between 1875 and 1910, when the last of the Alta mines closed down, sixty-seven more died from the same cause. Nor was Alta unique. At 7:30 A.M. on the morning of February 28, 1902, a slide tore away part of the workings of the Liberty Bell mine above Telluride. As rescuers toiled up from town, a second avalanche dropped on them. And finally, after the rescue work had ended and the weary volunteers were dragging the corpses and the injured back to town on sleds, there was a third slide. The triple blows killed nineteen men, including my grandfather's brother, and cruelly hurt eleven more. My stepfather-to-be saved himself by seizing a tree as he was being hurled down a hillside; there he clung, semiconscious, deafened and almost suffocated by the snow that had packed like cement into his ears, mouth, and nose.

At a mine where I had once worked above Ouray, a slide swept away the boardinghouse and killed seven or eight of my erstwhile companions. And we all listened to men like Harry Johnson, who had been trapped above Telluride at the Black Bear mine, where the cook and her husband had been crushed to death in their own bed; Johnson's tale of a dazed groping for help in the white wastes twelve thousand feet high was by no means reassuring.

As skiers unfamiliar with the slopes began thronging them, the Forest Service, which issued special-use permits for lifts that might carry the newcomers to disaster, took to worrying. The result was the establishment at Alta, during the winter of 1937–38, of the nation's first avalanche-research center. The masses of information collected there during subsequent years enabled not only ski patrols but also highway departments and telephone and pipeline maintenance crews to design protective bunkers at vulnerable spots, to predict unstable conditions, to shoot down threatening accumulations of snow with cannons and special "ava-

launchers." Today, if hazards warrant, slopes and highways are closed entirely, and when accidents do occur, tested rescue procedures are put into operation immediately. The results have been phenomenal. By 1965 the annual toll from avalanches, which once had killed a score or more people in the Rockies each year, had dropped to less than six, although more users than ever were travelling the roads and coursing the slopes.

The guidelines for whatever the Forest Service did, whether promoting outdoor sports or developing utilitarian goals, were laid down as matters of administrative policy by the Department of Agriculture and hence were susceptible to amendment with each change of administrators. To give the programs the dignity and stability of law, Congress in 1960 passed the Multiple Use-Sustained Yield Act. In this new act, recreational facilities were officially recognized for the first time as a national resource, and the service was ordered to "manage" recreation along with trees and grass and water.

Budgets jumped; crash programs were instituted. Thousands of miles of road were built not only for timber cutters and stockmen, as in the past, but also for growing numbers of highly sophisticated mobile camping units. Visitor information centers, built in imitation of similar units in the national parks, appeared in the more popular areas. Signs interpreting a region's history, geology, ecology, and whatnot sprang up beside the mountain highways. "Adventure" trails led from parking places into choice dells where viewers might glimpse animals in their native habitats.

Census takers meanwhile stalked the gathering places with clipboards and pencils, trying to determine what the forest visitors really wanted. Most, it seemed, were not touring the forests per se but were passing through on the way to visit relatives in another part of the country. They would leave the direct route if roads were good and afforded roomy turnouts where they could exclaim over striking views with a minimum of inconvenience. Fishermen among them hoped to be able to catch trout from the shoulder of the road and apparently saw no incongruity in ganging up elbow to elbow beside the pools formed by bridge abutments. A significant majority of the passersby insisted that when they "camped out" for a night in a mobile home, they preferred doing it in tight clusters with others of their kind. They desired showers and laundromats with hot and cold running water, sturdy tables and prepared fireplaces, convenient toilets and ready access to grocery stores and gasoline stations. When they returned at night from a day with the power boats or motor scooters that they carried with them, they were not averse to nearby entertainment—jukeboxes, bowling alleys, shooting galleries, cocktail lounges, and the like.

As more and more camping spots of this sort appeared, dissident voices began to sound. As long ago as 1872 naturalist John Muir of California's Sierra Nevada had spat out in a private letter that "rough vertical animals called men . . . occur in and on these mountains like sticks of condensed filth." But were modern recreationists really so inured to urban crowding that they craved similar conditions in the mountains? Or were their attitudes being subtly guided by the purveyors of an annual four billion dollars' worth of trailers, boats, scooters, sports clothing, and sports equipment—a new breed of exploiter as ruthless as any lumberman ever was?

Whatever the cause of the crowding—ignorance, exploitation, or inherent nastiness—its results were both disturbing and challenging to wilderness lovers. "We are entering a new era in land management," said an angry conservationist at a statewide Recreation Planning Conference at Missoula in 1966. "Our burgeoning population is descending on every available acre to recreate. . . . An army of family campers . . . crowds our public campgrounds every summer and makes Times Square look like a Buddhist retreat. . . . When the last wilderness trail has been cemented over; when the outdoor toilets are in mile-long rows, as close as houses on a Philadelphia street; and when parking lots cover ninety-nine per cent of every park, what then?"

One answer has been the closing of certain remote areas to roads and to all forms of commercial activity except some grazing. This is not a new movement. In 1924, Aldo Leopold of the Forest Service, an eloquent crusader for the concept of "quality" in outdoor recreation, prevailed on the government to set aside as the Gila Wilderness Area half a million acres of mountain land in southwestern New Mexico. Dozens of comparable reservations followed during the next decade —"wilderness areas" that were more than 100,000 acres in size; "wild areas" that were smaller; "primitive areas" in which limited amounts of lumbering, foraging, and water extraction might be allowed at some future date—a total of some 15,000,000 acres.

Like other Forest Service activities prior to 1960, the preservation of these wilderness regions was a matter of administrative policy and hence subject to arbitrary change. As pressures on the forests increased, wilderness-lovers began to fear that such changes would occur, and they attacked along a broad front, insisting that the entire wilderness system be given the protection of law.

An intense emotionalism accompanied the campaign. The wilderness, its proponents argued, was a priceless heritage—the land as our pioneers had known it—and it filled a spiritual need even for people who never saw it but derived abiding satisfaction just from knowing that it was there. Those who did seek it out found the country's last true solitude, with its powers to restore and sustain. There, somehow, was the embodiment of what Thoreau had meant with his paradoxical statement that "in wildness is the preservation of the world."

To many mountain dwellers that kind of thinking was incomprehensible. Grazing and timber lands, they said, ought to be utilized under the sustained-yield program. Though lumbering caused temporary scars, eventually the land could be made more beautiful than before through scientific reforestation. Emotionalism appeared in these arguments, too. One Colorado congressman scornfully labelled the preservationists "the deep breathers." Local businessmen trotted out a cliché as hoary as Thoreau's: "The economic strength of any nation lies in the exploitation of its natural resources." Wilderness bills were decried as class legislation—"the domination," said one Colorado lumberman, "of Public Land Use by . . . a minority group of the participants," and hence un-American.

The preservationists won. In September of 1964 President Johnson signed a bill that officially described the wilderness as "an area where the earth and its community of life are untrammeled by man, where man himself is a visitor who does not remain." More than 9,000,000 acres of former wild, wilderness, and "canoe" areas were placed within a National Wilderness Preservation System, to be managed in such a way as to keep them untrammelled by man—a paradox in itself, since the very word "management" is a denial of wilderness. Another five and a half million acres of erstwhile primitive areas were to be re-examined within ten years to determine whether they merited inclusion within the preservation system. Finally, methods were outlined whereby additional areas could be added to the total.

Within less than three years some three dozen proposals for additions had been offered to Congress. Men who looked on the forests as utilitarian objects wrung their hands. "Some of our esteemed citizens," wrote "Uncle Dudley" in *Nation's Agriculture* (July–August 1967), "are going a little nuts about wilder-

ness. Why, we just got done changing a wilderness into a fairly desirable United States of America." Anyway, most vacationists preferred the outdoors without primitiveness: "There is no waiting list," Uncle Dudley snorted, "for the unimproved camp sites!" Enough was enough.

So. The rush of recreationists to the Rockies looks like a new stampede, but in many ways it is a disturbingly familiar continuation of the old story of brutal exploitation. For example:

Not long ago, my family and I, travelling on horseback with friends, rode up Henson Creek above Lake City to American Flats, 12,000 feet high, mile upon mile of alpine tundra rolling around the feet of towering peaks. Scars showed everywhere—colored splotches of waste rock beside old prospect holes, a network of paths eroded into the thin, friable soil by uncounted numbers of sheep, the slash of a mine road climbing across a distant pass. A bruised land—but the wind sang, the cumulus clouds piled dazzlingly. An occasional jeep ground past, following the mine road, its sunburned occupants staring wide-eyed. A family banged along on two motor scooters, children clinging to their parents' waists; probably they lacked money for jeep rentals, or time or experience for horses, and this was the only way for them to see the highlands. Red flags fluttering from short yellow stakes showed where surveyors were contemplating a normal highway that would enable still more visitors to partake of the scene.

Then we veered away from the sheep trails and the roads, following the old Horsethief Trail through a gap in the rim. During the 1880's enterprising rustlers had stolen horses and mules in Lake City, had driven them across this breathless route to sell them in Ouray —then had doubled their profits by stealing more stock in Ouray for sale back in Lake City.

Behind us, Coxcomb Peak rose like a cleaver, Wetterhorn like a chisel snout. Ahead yawned Uncompahgre Canyon, 6,000 feet of blue-misted space from the top of Potosi down to the town of Ouray in the canyon bottom. High-antlered deer trotted along the near skyline, watching us as curiously as we watched them. One by one our horses came abruptly off a shale bank onto a sharp gray ridge. We rode dumbly, looking left into the stupendous gash of Uncompahgre gorge; and all at once, under our right boot toes, as startling as a yell in the night, gaped the Cow Creek drop we had forgotten about, one more mile of collapsing cliffs and trees and tormented ravines sliding down, down, down, to soar again on the opposite side to the stark cliffs of Courthouse Mountain.

Long ago someone had named that knife-edged ridge between the chasms the Bridge of Heaven. We held our breath as the horses walked gingerly across. Devilish things had reputedly happened there in the past. Wind had blown one prospector off to his death below. Lightning had killed another. A sheepherder, crossing the narrows in company with a rival in romance, had given the fellow a push. Or so they say. We zigzagged down among stately blue spruce, through asters and paintbrush and grass as high as our stirrups, past deep-blue larkspur, among white aspen boles, lost in a murmur that we called silence but that in reality was only the absence of human sound. Early the next morning we drove from Ouray up the winding highway to the south. High above the town, we pulled out on an overlook and studied the northeastern rim of the gigantic amphitheatre of cliffs, hoping to spot some part of the trail we had followed the day before. There? Or there? We could not be sure—so tiny a thread in the vastness.

"Never mind," my wife said. "We'll remember: all of it was a bridge of heaven."

Our eyes dropped back to the town. Red sight-seeing jeeps were leaving the garages to pick up the day's passengers. The strident thrum of a motorcycle reached even to where we stood. A huge sign, which we knew glared with lights by night, was stretched across a cliff face, showing the way to a local scenic wonder that everyone was invited to see—for a price. To the right, a large white star and a large white cross gave manmade blessings to the dark spruce. Behind us, noisome as well as visual, a fluff of smoke rose from the town dump, surely the loveliest dump site in the entire nation.

And above, in the high thin blueness, the Bridge of Heaven on Horsethief Trail. Four hundred years of it —the plunder trail to heart's desire. So it was for Coronado's Spaniards and William Ashley's beaver hunters, for the miners and the stockmen and the utopian colonists, for tie cutters and ditchdiggers. So, too, for today's vacationists and the purveyors who batten on them—there are, after all, more ways than one to skin either a cat or a continent.

The jeepsters sang and waved as they passed, and who is to say they were any less happy than the backpackers heading for the Mt. Hayden Hiking Trail, up Canyon Creek above the glaring sign? That's the hell of heaven: defining it to everyone's taste. Somehow, though, it has to be managed. For there simply are not four hundred more years of plunder remaining, either in the Rockies or in the country as a whole.

This sobering article about the transition of his native Rocky Mountain area from a mining to a tourist economy is based on a section of Mr. Lavender's new book, The Rockies, *recently published by Harper & Row.*

READING, WRITING, AND HISTORY

By BRUCE CATTON

U. S. Grant: *Man of Letters*

In the spring of 1885, when he was less than three months away from death by cancer, General Ulysses S. Grant had a spirited exchange of letters with Adam Badeau, who was supposed to be helping him write his memoirs.

Badeau had been Grant's military secretary during the final year of the Civil War, and some time after the war he had written a three-volume *Military History of Ulysses S. Grant.* This has been a standard reference work ever since, but it had not been a great commercial success and now it occurred to Badeau that it would sink into the shadows forever, once Grant's memoirs came out. Besides, to work on another man's manuscript struck Badeau as sheer drudgery, he saw his own name vanishing from sight under the great weight of Grant's name, and anyway he wanted to write a novel; so on May 2 he wrote to Grant demanding more money. Specifically, he wanted $1,000 a month, payable in advance, plus ten per cent of the entire profits from the memoirs.

Grant was combating poverty as well as cancer. The failure of the brokerage house of Grant & Ward had left him flat broke just at the moment he learned that the irritating sore in his throat that had bothered him so long was an inoperable cancer, and his one purpose now was to get royalties that would relieve his family from want. On May 5 he rejected Badeau's claim in the most plain-spoken terms—and in the course of

writing the letter unwittingly demonstrated that by the oddest turn of fate he had actually become what Badeau supposed himself to be: a man of letters.

Grant thought that Badeau was asking for altogether too much money, and said so flatly. What really irritated him, however, was Badeau's implication that Grant could not finish his book without Badeau's help. Grant's pride as a craftsman had been offended. He thought that his own literary style was good—a belief that was entirely justified—and in any case if a book came out with his name on it, it was going to be his book and nobody else's; he told Badeau that his conscience would not let him present a book as his work if he had not actually written it. His agonizing malady was now entering its terminal stage, he needed an amanuensis to help him organize some of the material, and he understood that he might die before the work was finished, in which case someone would have to arrange the final sections to make a coherent conclusion—but a ghost writer he did not want at all.

This is a little unexpected. Grant was a soldier; at one degree removed, he was a politician; and now he was writing a book, his only aim being to make money for his family. It should have been an open-and-shut case. If a hack could finish the job for him, well and good. It was clear by now that the book was going to sell very well indeed, and the money would come rolling in once the job was done and the door-to-door salesmen got busy. Why endure the work of composition—accompanied, as it must be in Grant's case, by the fearful pain of death-in-the-throat—when a journeyman like Badeau could do the work? Why, if money was all that mattered?

Obviously, money was not all that mattered. Grant wanted something more. He could no more take credit for a book he had not really written than he could have confessed that his Vicksburg campaign had been devised and executed by some subordinate. He had the pride of authorship. Badeau's financial terms were high, but by this time it was clear that they could be met without hardship. The real trouble was that Grant had become a writing man, and he was driven by the writing man's compulsions.

In his letter, Badeau had been fairly blunt. He complained that the work he was supposed to do for Grant would be "the merest literary drudgery," and went on:

In the nature of things, I can have no reputation and consideration from my connection with the book. I must efface myself, and yet work intensely hard without increased pay or any at all until a year and a half from the beginning of my labors. But your book has assumed an importance which neither you nor I anticipated last summer. It is to have a circulation of hundreds of thousands, and the larger its circulation the greater its importance—the more completely it will supplant and stamp out mine. The better I help you to make it, the more effectually I destroy what I have spent my life in building up—my reputation as your historian. And this nobody but me can do. No literary man has the military knowledge; no military man has the literary experiences; no literary or military man living, not one of your old Staff even, has one tithe of my knowledge and experience on this subject, the result of twenty years' study and devotion. . . . No one but myself can destroy my own book. If I don't help you it will retain its place, for you have neither the physical strength nor the habits of mind yourself to make the researches to verify or correct your own memory. If you can not finish the work, nobody can do it fitly but me.

Badeau had made a small mistake. He was writing to U. S. Grant, who was not used to being pushed around.

Grant replied: "I have concluded that you and I must give up all association so far as the preparation of any literary work goes which is to bear my signature. In all other respects I hope our relations may continue as they have always been, pleasant and friendly." He went on to say that the manuscript was by now much nearer completion than Badeau supposed, and he pointed out that the work required of the amanuensis would not be too extensive: "The work which I wanted you to do I did not think would take over two months of your time, working on an average of four hours a day, six days in the week. It would not take longer if done by an expeditious writer and as I want it done, and I thought and you thought the compensation large at the time." (Compensation: $5,000 out

of the first $20,000 in royalties, and $5,000 out of the next $10,000.)

Then Grant addressed himself to what seemed to be Badeau's chief complaint: that Grant's memoirs, once on sale, would bury Badeau's own work and sink Badeau's name in obscurity:

Allow me to say that this is all bosh, and evidently the work of a distempered mind that has been growing moody by too much reflection upon these matters. The fact is, if my book affects yours in any way it will be to call attention to it. You say that "I am a man of affairs, etc., and can tell a simple story," etc. You imply that a literary man must supply some deficiencies, and that you are the only man who can do it. If this is the case . . . I do not want a book bearing my name to go before the world which I did not write to such an extent as to be fully entitled to the credit of authorship. I do not want a secret between me and someone else which would destroy my honor if it were divulged. I cannot think of myself as depending upon any person to supply a capacity which I am lacking. I may fail, but I will not put myself in such a position.

You say, "no one but myself can destroy my own book. If I don't help you it will retain its place, for you have neither the physical strength," etc. In answer to this I have to say that for the last twenty-four years I have been very much employed in writing. As a soldier I wrote my own orders, plans of battle, instructions and reports. They were not edited, nor was assistance rendered. As president, I wrote every official document, I believe, usual for presidents to write, bearing my name. All these have been published and widely circulated. The public has become accustomed to my style of writing. They know that it is not even an attempt to imitate either a literary or classical style; that it is just what it is and nothing else. If I succeed in telling my story so that others can see as I do what I attempt to show, I will be satisfied. The reader must also be satisfied, for he knows from the beginning just what to expect.

The last two sentences of this paragraph add up to excellent advice for any budding writer. Grant capped them with a final declaration: "It would be a degradation for me to accept honors and profit from the work of another man while declaring to the public that it was the product of my own brain and hand."

In the upshot, Grant finished the job as he had said he would, and an examination of his original manuscript in the Library of Congress is instructive. In the final weeks, when he was almost distracted by unending pain, Grant's writing becomes a scrawl, disconnected episodes and comments are put down as they entered the man's head, and there is obvious reliance on an editor who can fit the separate pieces into their proper place and arrange the last chapter into a coherent tale. Yet with all of this it is fair to say that the manuscript required from the editor no more work than might be given to the manuscript of any professional writer who had been compelled by approaching death to leave his final pages in a slightly disorganized state. It might be added that Grant died just two days after he had written his final words.

The great bulk of the manuscript looks like a professional's work; which is to say that it contains the interlineations, the lines drawn through words and phrases, which show an unremitting effort to go over what has been written and find just the right way to say what the writer wanted said. Whether he did it well or poorly, Grant was behaving like a craftsman. . . . One more little touch. A few pages from the end, when the shadows were closing in fast, there is a page containing no writing at all—just doodles, a sketch of a farmhouse, a series of crosshatched squares and triangles: precisely the sort of byplay a writer indulges in when the next paragraph will not come out and the subconscious mind has to be given a chance to bring something to the surface. Grant was doodling, remember, at a time when simply to stay alive was torment and when the available time was short, but the job he was doing was of a kind that cannot always be hurried. Any writer will recognize the situation he was in.

If Grant thus finally became a literary man, the important question of course is: how good a literary man was he?

The answer is that he was surprisingly good. His *Personal Memoirs* stays alive and is read today, not simply because it recounts the wartime experiences of a famous soldier but primarily because it is a first-rate book—well written, with a literary quality that keeps it fresh. Mark Twain's famous verdict—that it is "a great, unique and unapproachable literary masterpiece"—is probably a little excessive, and yet the book has a quality that lifts it far above the other soldier-memoirs of its time and place. The English critic Matthew Arnold, no great admirer of Grant or of Americans generally, found Grant's literary style "straightforward, nervous, firm, possessing in general the high merit of saying clearly, in the fewest possible words, what had to be said, and saying it, frequently, with shrewd and unexpected turns of expression."

Grant was one of the most articulate of American soldiers. The prose style in which he took such pride is marked above all by clarity of expression. There is never any doubt about what Grant means, and this characteristic is visible in his wartime correspondence. His letters and orders are never foggy, and some of the most memorable sentences of the whole Civil War come straight from Grant's pen.

There is, for instance, his note to General Buckner: "No terms except unconditional and immediate surrender can be accepted. I propose to move immediately upon your works." And to Meade, outlining the

plan for the 1864 campaign: "Lee's army will be your objective point. Wherever Lee goes, there you will go also." Not to mention the note to Halleck, after Spotsylvania: "I propose to fight it out on this line if it takes all summer." In this one, it is interesting to notice that Grant originally wrote "if it takes me all summer" and then went back and crossed out the word "me"; he was the stylist even then, knocking out one word in order to make a sentence more effective.

In his private correspondence, Grant was careless. Spelling was a minor bother to him—not because he did not know how to spell, but apparently because he just didn't care much about it. It is common to find him spelling a word one way in one sentence and another way in the next one. He often wrote to his political sponsor, Congressman Elihu Washburne of Illinois, and he was quite capable of spelling Washburne's name both with and without the final *e* in the same letter. Once during the war he wrote to his twelve-year-old son Fred, from whom he had just had a letter, advising the young man to keep a dictionary with him when he wrote letters so that he could check his spelling; but like many another father, Grant preached what he did not himself practice. One of his aides, Horace Porter, wrote that Grant never had a dictionary in his tent, never bothered to write a word out on a scrap of paper to see if he had it right, and altogether spelled "with a heroic audacity."

But that was for private letters. Otherwise Grant used care, and long before he ever thought of writing his memoirs he took a modest pride in his writing style. His chief of staff, John A. Rawlins, in the winter of 1864 complained that to get Grant's report of the battle of Chattanooga into final shape "is a very unpleasant and I may say thankless undertaking, for the General is very tenacious of the claim that he writes his own reports and it is necessary for us to follow the text as nearly as possible." Inasmuch as Rawlins' own literary style was atrocious, one can only add that

General Grant was well advised to impose this rule.

All in all, Grant emerges as a man of letters of real distinction. Go back, again, to his performance in the *Memoirs*. He wrote this book against pain and death, and he stuck to it as long as he could hold a pencil—not because someone else could not finish the thing for him, thereby assuring his family a proper estate, but simply because as a writing man he wanted the book done his way. No professional author could have written a sturdier declaration of dedication to his craft: "I do not want a book bearing my name to go before the world which I did not write to such an extent as to be fully entitled to the credit of authorship."

KEEP THE CAMERAS ROLLING!

CONTINUED FROM PAGE 44

One after another the group began to succumb to sunstroke or malaria.

Through all this, liquor was the one sustainer. Renaldo followed the prescription given him by one of the white hunters, Pete Pearson, who had been in Africa for years: three fingers of Scotch—good Scotch —in the morning and three fingers at night. The idea was to keep the blood racing at such a pace that malaria would not have a chance to catch hold. Whatever the medical explanation, Renaldo never got sick.

"The person who suffered the most was Edwina," he said. "Blondes are particularly vulnerable to the sun. In Edwina it caused a kind of anemia." She was weak and listless eighty per cent of the time, but she rarely complained. "She had courage," said Olive, and John McClain agreed: "She had plenty of moxie. She went on with the work."

One day when they were shooting, the sky began to darken. One of the white hunters cried out: "Locusts!" They came in clouds, in the billions. It was like twilight at midday. The people ran for the tents and closed the flaps. When the swarm had passed, the trees were completely denuded—bare skeletons. The cameras and other equipment were caked with insects.

There was trouble in screening the rushes at night. The light attracted thousands of white flying ants—a great delicacy for the natives. As the ants settled on the screen the natives would fall on them and, despite repeated warnings, tear great holes in the screen.

What could have been a most tragic mishap came in the middle of the night. It had been raining heavily, and the cast and crew woke to find water seeping

under their tents. Then they heard a noise that was different from that of the falls. "Get to high ground," someone shouted, and the company fled—in nightclothes—to the hills in back of the camp. They had just reached them when a six-foot wall of water engulfed the camp, sweeping tents, food, and equipment into the river. All shooting had to be stopped until the safari could be refitted.

There were dangers during some of the actual shooting. For example, the script called for Olive's body to be found floating in the river just below the falls. The water was teeming with crocodiles, but Olive obligingly immersed herself while five hunters held their guns on the crocodiles, which were watching some fifty feet away. Suddenly an eddy caught her body and pushed it out from shore. She made no sound or move because she didn't want to spoil a take. "Cut!" cried Van Dyke, and the men reached her just as the crocodiles began closing in.

One member of the crew, a native boy, fell into the river and a crocodile ate him, before the horrified gaze of the film crew. After that, Van Dyke instructed the cameramen to keep their cameras ready at all times and to keep filming no matter what happened.

At one point, Van Dyke decided that a rhino charge would make a stirring scene. "Unfortunately," Renaldo said, "a rhino caught our scent and charged before we were prepared. Harry Carey jumped into a ditch and the rhino went right over his head. I leaped for a thorn tree and got punctured all over by those three- or four-inch thorns. As I bled away, pandemonium broke out below me. The hunters couldn't get a shot because the rhino was charging around among the crew. One native boy saw the rhino coming and just froze in terror. The rhino hit him straight on; he was dead before he hit the ground. The cameramen —on a raised platform out of harm's way—stuck to their cameras and got the entire action."

One sequence called for Carey, Edwina, and Renaldo, fleeing from natives and on the point of starvation, to come upon three lions feeding on a kill. So desperate is their plight, so agonizing their hunger, that they advance on the lions and drive them away with sticks and stones, as they would stray dogs. Then they fall on the kill themselves and gorge.

The white hunters scouted around until they found three lions tearing into a topi they had just dragged down. Van Dyke wrote later: "I ordered them [the actors] to charge [the lions] and drive [them] off the carcass, and the idiots did." It's in the picture.

Another scene called for Carey and Renaldo, again pursued by natives, to swing through overhead vines to an island in a small lake alive with crocodiles.

Van Dyke and his men diverted part of the river into a pond, threw carrion into it to lure the crocodiles, and then constructed a heavy gate to close them in. Some two hundred were thus trapped. The following two days were overcast, however, and the creatures had to be kept penned up waiting for sunny shooting weather. At night the crocodiles would charge the gate and, to keep them from escaping, the entire company would thrust burning torches down their throats. The director later wrote:

... the eyes of the crocodiles would stand out a fiery red ... until they made the rush, emerging from the water onto dry land, and they came fast, darting like lizards, and were always almost upon us before we were set for the shock of their attack.

Miss Booth, who was on one of the shifts and fighting side by side with the men, had nearly fallen inside the fence while trying to ram a stick down a charging croc's throat. The tail of a croc had blasted its way through the fence at one spot and, catching Harry Carey on the leg, practically laid him up for a week.

Pete Pearson whispered to another white hunter during the fray: "These people are absolutely crackers."

Miss Booth was a constant miracle to the natives. At one spot, in the Ituri Forest of the Congo, the company met natives who had never seen a white woman before. They would not approach her or touch her, but they would stare at her for hours. To show signs of approval they made a strange guttural cluck-clucking deep in their throats. One day about two hundred natives decided to honor her with a dance. They assembled before her tent, and, of course, she had to come out. They were hot and perspiring, and it was high noon. They danced on and on—for three hours—but she smiled through it.

Renaldo had his adventures, too. "He was always going off on side trips," Olive said, "and this made Van furious." One day he went on a hunt with some

Pygmies who got their meat by sneaking up on an elephant and cutting its leg tendons. The animal then collapsed and the Pygmies fell on him with their knives and hatchets and clubs. "I have seen them carve living hunks of meat from the animal," said Renaldo, "and eat it on the spot."

He was made a blood brother of the Masai tribe, and still has a scar on his left wrist where blood was drawn. He pressed his wrist to the bloody wrist of a Masai warrior, and then drank the ceremonial draught of milk and cow's blood.

Of all the places the unit visited, the most memorable was the "Mountains of the Moon," on the boundary between the Congo and Uganda. "Everything there is out of proportion," Renaldo said. "A fruit tree is not ten feet high but fifty. The leaf of a sunflower is six feet in diameter. You can smell the frangipani three or four miles away, and if you are near it, the aroma is so powerful that you get drowsy."

But what the actors remember most vividly about Africa is "that clear light, that intense peace, that stillness of countryside, of flat-topped trees so delicate, with the mountains in the background shimmering in the heat haze."

But for all that, things were not going well with the movie makers. Olive had to be taken to Nairobi for an emergency operation, and the script girl came down with a serious case of malaria. Van Dyke himself was not well. He had suffered attacks of malaria and had developed a severe hacking cough that went on for minutes at a time each morning. As for Edwina, she was hardly seen at the end of the day; looking ever weaker, she would disappear into her tent.

A few personal relationships were beginning to fray; tempers were getting shorter, and there was too much drinking. When Van Dyke went out for a day's shooting, his water bottle was often filled with gin. Word must have reached the home office, because an order (of questionable enforceability) came through that if anyone were seen with liquor he would be fired.

It was becoming difficult to start the day. Van Dyke later wrote: "You'd crawl out of your tent every morning and say 'Oh, God, do I have to look at that face again and listen to its chatter again?'"

One day, after hours of shooting in the broiling sun, Van Dyke ordered Edwina to climb into a tree—

the scene called for lions to prowl around the trunk as she cringed among the branches. While in the tree, she fainted and fell to the ground. Luckily, there were no lions nearby, but Renaldo lost control of himself and ran up to Van Dyke shouting, "You son of a bitch, I'm going to kill you." Members of the company intervened, but the incident was like the tolling of a bell, and they all knew it was time for them to get out.

Then came a cable from Metro that said, in effect: come home now or don't bother to come at all. Van Dyke had shot almost five million feet of film, had been in Africa almost a year, covering forty thousand square miles of bush and jungle, and had exceeded his budget by almost a million dollars.

The unit broke up at Thika Falls, near Nairobi. The actors and most of the crew headed for Mombasa and home, while Van Dyke remained a few weeks to get still more scenic shots. There was a farewell party that lasted all night. Everyone wept, swore eternal friendship, and agreed that no other group could have done what they had done.

Back in Hollywood, they found themselves in a new jungle, this one of problems. First, all production stopped for six months while editors tried to cut five million feet of film to fit the story line. There were gaps where the sound was insufficient, and M.G.M., nervous about the strange new medium of talking pictures, decided that these scenes had to be reshot under the guidance of a dialogue coach and a stage director imported from New York.

To redo some of Olive's scenes, M.G.M. hired the famous Marjorie Rambeau at a thousand dollars a day. After several days someone realized that the public knew Miss Rambeau had not been on the trip to Africa. There was much consternation and confusion; finally Irving Thalberg asked Olive if she would redo her own scenes. She said she would be glad to—for a thousand dollars a day. The studio reluctantly agreed.

The new director from New York decided to take the actors to Tecate, Mexico, where he constructed an enormous animal compound and stocked it with wildlife: monkeys, panthers, leopards, lions, and elephants. Then he dug a ditch around the compound so the cameras could peer discreetly in at the animals.

When all was ready, Renaldo entered the compound to do a scene wherein he was to fondle the head of an ostrich. The bird didn't like it and ran away. This startled a leopard, which leapt onto an elephant. "All

hell broke loose," said Renaldo. "It was the most bloody massacre I've ever seen. Those animals ate each other up or clawed each other to death. And not a single foot of film was any good. They had buried the cameras too low and all we saw at the rushes was a dust cloud and now and then a leg kicking. There went the animals—and some three hundred thousand dollars."

Then came a disconcerting discovery: because of chemical differences in the water used in developing, all the reshot film was unusable because it did not match the film shot in Africa.

By this time M.G.M. officials were getting quite ugly, and it was rumored that they were going to abandon the picture entirely. "You see," Olive said, "they still didn't realize what they had in that movie."

William Randolph Hearst had invested in the picture. One night Renaldo dined with Hearst at San Simeon; the actor spoke so enthusiastically about their adventures and about his faith in the picture that Hearst put in a call to someone—he didn't say who—in New York. "The picture must go on as intended, financed as intended. That is all," said Hearst.

After that—and possibly because of it—Van Dyke was reinstated as director. The original sound was doctored up so that what the audience eventually saw was the movie with both the original film and sound, except for a few closeups between Edwina and Renaldo.

In the long run most of that extraordinary five million feet of film was used in one way or another. For years afterward, *Trader Horn* footage showed up as intercuts in Tarzan movies. Renaldo laughed about it: "How often I've been watching Johnny Weissmuller and Red Corrigan—who was always in the gorilla suit—when suddenly there would be an intercut and there I'd be or Edwina or Olive way off in the distance, walking through the jungle." Olive added, "M.G.M. made as much money selling surplus film of *Trader Horn* as they did from the movie itself." Reportedly, the price was ten dollars a foot.

Trader Horn not only made money; the landscape was so beautifully portrayed that it also made people want to see Africa for themselves. About a year after the movie opened, one of Renaldo's white-hunter friends wrote to him: "Business generally jumped 100% since you were here and the safari business has leaped about 1,000%."

Trader Horn was followed by a spate of jungle films. More important, the movie had an influence on Ernest Hemingway. "When I saw *Trader Horn* with all that magnificent *paysage* which the camera caught, I really got interested in Africa," he once told Renaldo.

Back in the United States, Edwina was genuinely ill, with a disease that defied diagnosis, and after a few years she sued the studio for millions. She lost the suit,

102

but according to rumor the studio gave her about twenty thousand dollars. After the lawsuit, Van Dyke, Carey, and Renaldo collected money for Edwina—she was swamped with lawyers' and doctors' bills—and sent it to her anonymously. "Even when she was working, she was shamefully underpaid," Renaldo commented. "Harry Carey and I were getting about six hundred dollars a week. Edwina was hired at seventy-five dollars a week."

Van Dyke lived for another ten years and directed some excellent motion pictures (among them *Naughty Marietta*). But the hazards of filming *Trader Horn* may well have shortened his life.

Renaldo made few pictures during the thirties and forties, but later he did play the title role in *The Cisco Kid;* from this and television serials, he made a comfortable living.

"I don't know why we didn't keep in touch with Edwina," Olive said to me. "When I knew you were coming I rummaged around and found a phone number someone gave me about a year ago." She went into another room and came back with a scrap of paper. "It's supposed to be Edwina's," she said, handing it to me. It was a number in a large western city.

I was about to put in the call when I said to Renaldo: "Here. You do it." We were all suddenly uneasy. It didn't seem possible that after all these years she could be found just by picking up the phone.

Renaldo dialed the number, and we waited. Someone answered, and, after thirty-four years, he smiled in instant recognition. "Edwina," he said, "this is Duncan." There was a little gasp at the other end. "Duncan," said a light, charming voice. "How are you?"

"Where have you been?" he asked. "We thought you were dead."

"I know," she replied rather sadly. "I know people think that, but that's all right with me. Let them keep thinking it."

She explained that she had married and that her husband had several children by a previous marriage. Like her, he was a Mormon. They lived quietly, she said, and their lives revolved around church work. Few of her friends knew who she really was and she wanted to keep her past life a secret, even now.

A few minutes later, Renaldo said good-bye and hung up. "I don't altogether understand Edwina," he said. "Although she was a very determined young woman, she was naïve. She thought that good work and honest effort are always justly rewarded. She had worked so hard, under such difficult conditions, she felt she deserved better treatment than she got. We all think so, too. But instead of accepting it gracefully, Edwina, I think, has just tried to blank out her whole life during those years."

But surely neither she nor any of them can ever forget. Certainly not Olive, whose grandchildren love to hear about the time Granny went into the jungles of Africa. And it is probable that even Edwina must occasionally take pride in recalling how she attacked lions with a stick, how she fought a raging crocodile, and how, surrounded by a thousand awestruck subjects, she was for a time a beautiful fair-haired goddess.

Mr. Riggan, affiliated with the Great Books Foundation in Chicago, has been a film buff ever since the day he auditioned for M.G.M. as a boy soprano. He didn't get the role.

A DIM VIEW OF PRESIDENTIAL PROSPECTS

JEFFERSON

Timothy Pickering and Richard Peters were both prominent patriots and members of the Continental Congress's "board of war" during the Revolution. By 1806 both were ardent Federalists, and on April 13 of that year Pickering wrote Peters a letter that included this passage:

If Jefferson had not been five years our President, I should not have believed it possible for one man, controuled by precise constitutional rules and laws, to produce such a revolution in politics and morals as we now see. . . . The national spirit and dignity are gone—never to rise while Jefferson bears rule. And who will succeed? A man of character & ability? No! The feeble, timid Madison, or the dull Monroe. . . . Fools and knaves will continue to be the general favourites of the people, until the government is subverted.

From *Essex Institute Historical Collections*, October, 1958

MADISON

MONROE

lis, who that year was running for the U.S. Senate.

When the platform reached the floor of the convention, Humphrey presented a minority report urging adoption of a stronger civil-rights plank and demanded a roll-call vote. After a tumultuous floor fight, the liberals carried the day, 651½ to 582½. Immediately, thirty-five delegates from Mississippi and Alabama stalked out of the convention—and the party—in protest. But the majority of southern delegates, however dejected they felt, stayed in their seats.

As for Truman, although his plans had gone awry the convention's decision was hardly unacceptable. The new civil-rights plank echoed many of the proposals that he himself had made to Congress in February in his special civil-rights message. In his memoirs, Truman proudly cites an exchange between a newsman and South Carolina's Governor J. Strom Thurmond on the convention floor. "President Truman is only following the platform that Roosevelt advocated," the reporter pointed out. "I agree," Thurmond replied. "But Truman really *means* it."

At last the convention had come to its main order of business, the nomination of a presidential candidate. The southern delegates remaining at the convention threw their support behind Senator Richard Russell of Georgia. But it was a token gesture. On the first roll call, Russell received only 263 votes. Truman got 947½ and the nomination.

It was nearly two o'clock in the morning when the balloting ended and Democratic National Chairman J. Howard McGrath sought out the candidate, who was waiting in the wings. Did the President want a recess until a more civilized hour the next night? In a few moments McGrath returned to the platform with the answer. "The boss doesn't want to wait," said McGrath. "He wants to get at them as soon as he can."

And get at them he did. Marching jauntily into the stifling heat of the auditorium, Truman waited until the welcoming demonstration subsided and then brought the delegates right back to their feet with his opening thrust. "Senator Barkley and I will win this election and make these Republicans like it," the President declared. "Don't you forget that."

For the moment at least, the delegates seemed to believe him. They stomped and cheered as he reeled off a long list of Democratic achievements and again lashed out at the sins of the Republican Congress. Then, building toward his climax, he noted that the platform adopted by the Republican convention favored legislation to remedy the housing shortage, curb

inflation, and increase social security benefits. The Eightieth Congress, he charged, had failed to act on these and other worthy proposals. Finally, Truman dropped his bombshell:

On the twenty-sixth day of July, which out in Missouri we call "Turnip Day," I am going to call Congress back and ask them to pass laws to halt rising prices, to meet the housing crisis—which they are saying they are for in their platform.... They can do this job in fifteen days, if they want to do it. They will still have time to go out and run for office.*

In summoning Congress back to Capitol Hill before the election, Truman laid himself open to charges of playing politics, a point the Republicans were prompt to press home. Then too, there was always the chance that the Republican congressional leadership would push through the legislation Truman proposed, and take credit for it. But Truman believed he had no choice. As Clark Clifford, the suave St. Louis lawyer (now Secretary of Defense) who was the President's top political adviser throughout the campaign, put it: "We've got our backs on our own one-yard line with a minute to play; it has to be razzle-dazzle." Moreover, Truman was confident that the Republicans would not call his bluff. "Of course I knew," he wrote later, "that the special session would produce no results in the way of legislation."

The Congress fulfilled his expectations. The grumbling lawmakers authorized a loan to help the United Nations build its new headquarters in New York, but did nothing substantial about inflation, the housing shortage, civil rights, or the other major problems of the day. Less than two weeks later, the Republican leaders closed up shop and went home, leaving behind a fresh supply of ammunition for Truman.

Only a few weeks remained before Labor Day, the official start of the campaign. Truman began working out the details of the battle plan with his staff. Clifford was the President's first deputy and chief speech writer. Louis Johnson, a wealthy Washington attorney, took over the thankless and unwanted post of finance chairman. Along with Chairman McGrath, Matt Connelly, the President's appointments secretary, handled liaison with local politicians around the country. No one held the title of campaign manager, but everyone knew who was in charge. It was, of course, the President.

In August, as these men made their plans, the Democratic situation seemed blacker than ever. The hope

* "Turnip Day" has no legal status in Missouri or anywhere else. In fact few Missourians had even heard of it until the President brought it up. But oldtimers explained that it was a day set aside for planting turnips so they would have time to mature before the first frost. One seed company reported that after Truman's reminder, its sales of turnip seed suddenly tripled.

that had flickered at the Philadelphia convention had been extinguished almost immediately when southern Democrats, rebelling against the party's strong civil-rights plank, held a convention of their own in Birmingham, Alabama. The Dixiecrats, as they were dubbed, nominated Thurmond as their presidential candidate and Governor Fielding L. Wright of Mississippi as his running mate. Their platform made plain what they regarded as the main issue of the campaign: "We stand for the segregation of the races and the racial integrity of each race."

A few days after the Dixiecrats adjourned, Henry Wallace's Progressive party convened in Philadelphia. There, in the same hall used by the Democrats and Republicans, the Progressives formalized the nominations (actually decided on months before) of Wallace for President and Democratic Senator Glen Taylor of Idaho for Vice President. "The party Jefferson founded 150 years ago was buried here in Philadelphia last week," Wallace declared. "But the spirit which animated that party in the days of Jefferson," Wallace claimed, now infused his own Progressive movement.

The Dixiecrats and the Progressives threatened to make major inroads among normally Democratic voters. Nevertheless, Truman and his aides decided that for the most part they would ignore the two splinter parties. The President's only chance of victory, they concluded, was in mounting an all-out attack against the Republicans. They had already chosen the Eightieth Congress as the chief target for the assault. Now they focused their attack on two important, sensitive areas: labor and farm legislation.

Truman's first salvo came at the Democrats' opening Labor Day rally in Detroit's Cadillac Square. The President had good reason to claim labor's friendship. In June, 1947, he had vetoed the Taft-Hartley Bill, which most union men regarded as an abridgement of the rights they had fought for so hard during the turbulent 1930's. His reception in the strongest union town in the country showed that organized labor had not forgotten. Crowds lined the streets six to ten deep along his route from the rail terminal to Cadillac Square, where some 175,000 people waited to hear him.

In his nationally broadcast speech, the President lost no time in bringing up Taft-Hartley, which, as he reminded his listeners, the Eightieth Congress had promptly passed over his veto. "If the congressional elements that made the Taft-Hartley law are allowed to remain in power," Truman warned, "... you men of labor can expect to be hit by a steady barrage of body blows. And if you stay at home, as you did in 1946, and keep these reactionaries in power, you will deserve every blow you get." A Republican victory, the President went on, threatened the welfare of the

In his coverage of the GOP convention, British caricaturist David Low anticipated the role that television would soon play in presidential politics.

entire nation. "I would fear not only for the wages and living standards of the American workingman, but even for our democratic institutions of free labor and free enterprise." The President obviously was swinging wildly. But judging from the cheers and shouts of "Give 'em hell, Harry!" that went up from the crowd, some of his blows were striking home.

From organized labor and its discontent with Taft-Hartley, Truman now turned his attention to the farmers, who had their own reasons for grumbling that year. All summer, grain prices had been dropping steeply; corn, for example, had fallen from $2.46 a bushel in January to $1.78 in September. Blaming the Eightieth Congress for the price slide was more complicated than blaming it for the Taft-Hartley Act, but Truman managed to do it.

The basis of the farmer's trouble was the enormous crop surplus produced in 1948. Ordinarily, the farmer could store his surplus grain in government silos until prices rose, when he could sell it at a profit on the open market; the federal government, or more specifically the Commodity Credit Corporation, loaned the farmer money on the crops stored. But in renewing the C.C.C.'s authorization in 1948, Congress failed to give it the power to acquire additional storage bins. When the bumper 1948 harvests came in, the C.C.C. ran out of storage space and the farmers were forced to sell at the low market price.

The whole problem seems to have stemmed as much from oversight and confusion over the complexities of the farm program as from anything else. Truman had never raised the issue until the campaign. Now he brought it up in his first major farm speech, at the National Plowing Contest at Dexter, Iowa, on September 18. "This Republican Congress has already stuck a pitchfork in the farmer's back," the President declared. "They tied the hands of the administration. They are preventing us from setting up storage bins that you will need in order to get the support price for your grain." Whatever the oversimplifications of this argument, it had a powerful appeal to the farmers who were feeling the pinch of depressed grain prices.

Using the Taft-Hartley Law and the storage-bin issue like blunt weapons, the President swept across the land, bludgeoning the Republicans. He travelled in the Presidential Special, a seventeen-car train that also carried the press and a retinue of advisers and Secret Service men. A converted Pullman car, luxuriously fitted and protected with armor plate and bullet-proof glass, was set aside for the President, his wife, Bess, and his daughter, Margaret. The car was called the *Ferdinand Magellan,* and in it Truman covered more distance than the Portuguese explorer who circled the globe. Counting his "nonpolitical" trip to California in June, the President reckoned that he travelled 31,700 miles, made 356 prepared speeches and 200 more extemporaneous talks, and was seen by twelve to fifteen million people.

The scale of Truman's campaign was all the more remarkable for the fact that it was plagued by severe financial troubles. The overwhelming pessimism about Democratic chances cut the normal flow of campaign contributions down to a trickle. Finance Chairman Johnson was often forced to reach into his own pocket to meet day-to-day expenses. At the very start of the campaign, a radio network threatened to cancel the scheduled broadcast of the Labor Day speech unless it got its $50,000 payment in advance. But a last-minute phone call to Oklahoma Governor Roy Turner, who managed to raise the money in a few hours, saved the day.

As time went on, the Democrats learned to make a virtue of their financial adversity. On several occasions Johnson, to dramatize the party's financial plight, allowed the networks to cut the President off the air before he had finished a speech. Once, when a network official warned that Truman would be cut off unless the Democrats put up more money, Johnson told him: "Go ahead. That will mean another million votes."

The financial uncertainties contributed to the helter-skelter atmosphere that prevailed on the Presidential Special. "Things were done . . . as if we were operating just one jump ahead of the sheriff," Charles G. Ross, Truman's press secretary, recalled. "Many of the speeches were written as we went along. . . . We were understaffed. The White House girls sat up night after night, typing and retyping."

None of these practical problems seemed to discourage the candidate. He was too busy campaigning, and he got better at it as he went along. At first, his delivery of speeches was as unimpressive as always. But by early October, Truman was writing the final drafts of all his major speeches, shaping raw material provided by his staff to his own style. He abandoned attempts at rhetorical flourishes and relied on short, punchy sentences and straightforward construction. His delivery also became noticeably more relaxed and effective.

The President was at his best making brief impromptu speeches at whistle-stops along the way. After blazing away at the Republicans from the train's rear platform for ten or fifteen minutes, he would ask: "Howja like to meet the boss?" Then he would usher out Bess Truman, while the crowd applauded warmly. Next, with a sly wink, he would present "the boss's boss," and Margaret Truman would appear, to be greeted by more cheers and, occasionally, a wolf whistle. Day after day the President repeated this performance at country depots, sidings, and water tanks, wherever a crowd could be gathered. He averaged ten speeches a day, and one day he spoke sixteen times.

His staff and the newsmen complained of exhaustion, but the sixty-four-year-old Truman seemed to thrive on the hectic pace. He was plainly enjoying the battle, and even those who admired neither his politics nor his style had to respect his pluck. "I'm going to fight hard, and I'm going to give them hell," Truman vowed when the campaign began, and he was certainly doing that. But he had also pledged to make the campaign the most important "since the Lincoln-Douglas debates." It was a promise he was finding impossible to keep, because it takes two to debate, and the frustrating fact was that no matter how furiously he lashed out at the Republicans, the Republican candidate simply ignored him.

Dewey also was travelling around the country in a campaign train, the Victory Special, with his staff of experts and speech writers. The two men spoke at many of the same places. Judging from the tone of Dewey's utterances, however, he seemed to be conducting not an election campaign but rather a triumphant tour of good will.

Dewey's decision to give Truman the silent treatment was based on his firm conviction that his victory was all but certain. It was a reasonable conclusion, for every important indicator pointed in that direction. The most persuasive evidence was supplied by the major public-opinion polls conducted by George Gallup, Elmo Roper, and Archibald Crossley. Their surveys, which had correctly predicted the outcome of every presidential election since 1936, were regarded with unqualified awe. Ever since the nominating conventions, all three had predicted Dewey's victory. On September 9, Elmo Roper had blandly announced that "my whole inclination is to predict the election of **Thomas E. Dewey** by a heavy margin and devote my time and effort to other things." The fact that the campaign was barely a week old made little difference to Roper. "Past elections," he explained in his nationally syndicated newspaper column, "have shown us that normally there is little change in the final standings between early September and Election Day. Therefore, unless some major convulsion takes place in the next month and a half...Mr. Dewey is just as good as elected."

It was hard to find a dissenting opinion. Of America's newspapers, sixty-five per cent, representing nearly eighty per cent of the nation's total circulation, supported Dewey, and their editors and correspondents were confident they were backing a winner. In its October 11 issue, *Newsweek* published the results of a poll of fifty top political reporters, every one of whom predicted that Dewey would be the next President.

So overwhelming was the belief in a Republican victory that any evidence to the contrary was mistrusted and rejected. For example, the Staley Milling Company, a Kansas City feed supplier, conducted an informal poll of its customers that showed that fifty-four per cent of them preferred Truman to Dewey. The farmers registered their preference by buying sacks of chicken feed marked with either a donkey or an elephant. In September, after 20,000 farmers in six Midwestern states had been polled in this way, the company called off the survey. "We read the Gallup and Roper polls that were all for Dewey," a company official explained, "and we decided that our results were too improbable."

The same logic was used by the reporters accompanying Truman's campaign train when they discounted the significance of the large crowds that gathered to hear the President almost everywhere he spoke. Reporters who travelled with both candidates agreed that Truman was attracting much bigger audiences than Dewey, and some mentioned this puzzling phenomenon in their stories. The answer that satisfied them was that the voters were turning out to see President Truman and his family, rather than Democratic candidate Truman.

No wonder, then, that Dewey and his advisers found it easy to believe that the Presidency was within their grasp. Believing that, it was logical for them to reason that Dewey had nothing to gain and possibly a great deal to lose by hitting back at Truman. Such a response, the Dewey camp feared, would only lend credibility to the President's charges. Besides, Dewey and his advisers saw distinct advantages in conducting what

Pogo's *Walt Kelly envisioned Wallace being hit by his own campaign charges, Truman running blind, Dewey as a self-propelled adding machine, and Thurmond not at all.*

came to be called a "high level" campaign. By avoiding specific issues, Dewey could avoid antagonizing Republican conservatives, with whom he disagreed sharply on a broad range of foreign and domestic problems. By not committing himself to one policy or another, Dewey would also enjoy more flexibility in dealing with the nation and the world once he moved into the White House.

Accordingly, as Dewey's campaign train rolled across the nation (he travelled 18,000 miles and made 170 speeches), the candidate let fall one glittering generality after another. In Des Moines, where his campaign began, he pledged that "as President, every act of mine will be determined by one principle above all others: Is this good for our country?" And in Phoenix he candidly assured his audience that "your future is still ahead of you. And that's exactly what I believe about every part of our country. That's what I've been saying to our people."

Obviously there would have to be some changes made in the government, Dewey asserted. But when he talked about change he sounded more like an office manager than a potential chief of state. "We are going to have a big house-cleaning in Washington," he promised, "the biggest untangling, unsnarling, weed-

107

ing and pruning operation in our history." Over and over, Dewey stressed his main theme—national unity. "Our future and the peace of the world are staked on how united the people of America are," he proclaimed.

In the interest of unity, Dewey managed to take a remarkably tolerant view of Democratic sins. "I will not contend that all our difficulties today have been brought about by the present national administration," he said in Des Moines. "Some of these unhappy conditions are the results of circumstances beyond the control of any government."

The march of events in the summer of 1948 had presented the Republicans with singular opportunities to embarrass the Democratic administration. Abroad, the Russians launched their prolonged blockade of Berlin. Dewey was known to believe that the precarious Western position in Berlin was due in part to U.S. bungling at postwar international conferences. But after conferring with John Foster Dulles, one of his foreign-policy advisers, he decided not to make Berlin a campaign issue. Instead, he praised the Berlin airlift, ordered by Truman, as "proof of our determination to stand by the free peoples of Europe until united they can stand by themselves." As for Democratic blunders in foreign affairs, Dewey limited himself to casting passing slurs. "It wouldn't serve any useful purpose," he explained in his major foreign-policy address in Salt Lake City, "to recall tonight how the Soviet has conquered millions of people as the result of the failures of statesmanship."

At home, the House Un-American Activities Committee aired sensational charges of Communist espionage reaching into the upper echelons of government. Among the federal officials implicated in the Red spy ring by witnesses like Elizabeth T. Bentley and Whittaker Chambers were Harry Dexter White, former Assistant Secretary of the Treasury, and Alger Hiss, who as a State Department official had been instrumental in the establishment of the United Nations.

Truman promptly derided the charges as "a red herring." But the committee hearings made glaring headlines all summer long, and Americans, already fearful of the menace of Communist aggression overseas, were deeply disturbed about the suggestions of subversion at home.

Here was an issue, Republican National Chairman Hugh Scott argued, with which Dewey could set the prairies ablaze. But Dewey refused to get "panicky" about the Red threat. Instead of pounding away at Truman for negligence, he offered only mild reproofs, meanwhile promising a safe and sane solution to the Communist problem when he moved into the White House. "So long as we keep the Communists among us out in the open, in the light of day," he declared,

"the United States of America has nothing to fear from them within its own borders."

If there was little in Dewey's pronouncements to offend the voters, there was equally little to arouse their enthusiasm. Nor, for that matter, was the candidate's own personality the kind that moves multitudes. Dewey was the first presidential nominee to be born in the twentieth century, and he was very much a man of his age. Nearly everything he did, and the way he did it, crackled with modern efficiency.

The smooth routine aboard Dewey's Victory Special presented a sharp contrast with the slapdash operation of the Truman campaign. Every stopover and speech was carefully timed, and Dewey's staff saw to it that everything went off on schedule. For these technicians, no detail was too trifling. There was, for example, Mrs. Dewey's favorite hat, a red-felt affair with black trim. As attractive as the colors were to the eye, they did not photograph well. The problem was taken under advisement, and after duly discreet discussion, a compromise was worked out: Mrs. Dewey could wear the nonphotogenic hat at whistle-stops where there were no photographers; in the bigger towns she agreed to don something else before the flashbulbs started to pop.

The trouble with such precise planning was that when things occasionally did not go exactly according to blueprint, Dewey exhibited an all-too-obvious exasperation. Somewhere in Illinois, as Dewey began to speak, his train suddenly lurched backward a few feet, nearly injuring some bystanders. "Well, that's the first lunatic I've had for an engineer," the Governor exploded. "He probably should be shot at sunrise, but we'll let him off this time since no one was hurt."

Newsmen, bored with the awesome dullness of Republican efficiency and the lack of fresh fodder in Dewey's speeches, naturally seized upon the remark; and so, when he heard about it, did Truman. "We've had wonderful train crews, all across the country," the President declared, explaining that they "are all Democrats." The Republican candidate "objects to having engineers back up," Truman taunted. "He doesn't mention that under the great engineer [Herbert] Hoover, we backed up into the worst depression in history." It may provide some insight into Dewey's character that he denounced a careless railroad engineer yet held his temper under the rhetorical barrage fired at him by Truman.

Although the President never mentioned his opponent by name, his references were entirely clear. He called for an end to "mealy-mouth unity speeches" on domestic issues and jeered at Dewey's talk of bipartisan foreign policy. "The unity we have achieved required leadership," Truman said. "It was achieved by men—Republicans as well as Democrats—who were willing to fight for principles, not by the people who copied the answers down neatly after the teacher had written them on the blackboard."

In Pittsburgh, Truman complained that his opponent had "set himself up as a kind of doctor with a magic cure for all ills of mankind." Then Truman acted out a brief playlet in which the American people paid an office visit to Doctor Dewey for the "routine four-year check-up." Stroking an imaginary mustache in pantomime of young Doc Dewey, Truman prescribed a "special brand of soothing syrup—I call it unity." When the patient demanded to know exactly what was wrong, the Doctor replied: "I never discuss issues with a patient. What you need is a major operation."

Alarmed, the patient asked: "Will it be serious, Doc?"

"No," said the Doctor. "It will just mean taking out the complete works and putting in a Republican Administration."

This skit, written and performed by the President of the United States, was as close to a dialogue as the two major candidates were to come during the campaign.

As for the standard-bearers of the Progressive and the States' Rights parties, they also went their separate ways. In both cases, their courses seemed to take them further and further from the American mainstream. The Wallace party had begun with high hopes of waging a populist crusade that would gather support from the farm and labor groups which in the 1924 presidential election had rallied behind "Fighting Bob" La Follette of Wisconsin. But by his sweeping attacks on "Republican reaction," Truman had stolen most of the old populist thunder on domestic issues.

Wallace was left with only one main issue—peace. But in the summer of 1948, what Wallace called "peace" was regarded by many Americans as appeasement. Wallace's pleas for conciliation with the Soviet Union were undermined by the stark evidence of the Soviet's aggressive intentions: first the Communist coup in Czechoslovakia in February and then the Berlin blockade in June. Moreover, Wallace's refusal to disavow Communist support, and the prominent role Communists and their sympathizers played in the councils of the Progressive party, smeared his whole campaign with a Red brush.

The Dixiecrat insurgency was faring no better. To start with, Thurmond had been virtually assured thirty-eight electoral votes, in four southern states where the Democratic organizations had made him the party's official candidate. Striving to build on that

Confident of victory, Dewey studded his speeches with glittering generalities on the theme of "national unity."

foundation, Thurmond barnstormed through the South, evoking the spirit of the Confederacy with his battle cries of "racial purity" and "states' rights."

But even in the heart of Dixie, the old Rebel yells had lost much of their appeal. "We will pay through the nose for the Dixiecrats," warned the Atlanta *Constitution*, "as we still pay for the leadership which took us into the War Between the States to 'save us.' " Practical southerners, moreover, saw no point in hurting Truman to help Dewey, whose racial views were fully as abhorrent to them as the President's and whose party they intensely mistrusted.

The evidence that the Progressive and Dixiecrat campaigns were faltering was ignored by the pollsters, who insisted that Dewey would win no matter how the splinter parties fared. The final Gallup poll, just before the election, gave Truman 44.5 per cent of the vote, to 49.5 per cent for Dewey. Gamblers quoted odds of fifteen or twenty to one against the President, and the verdict of Democratic state leaders just before the election was: "In the time left, he can't make it."

As the campaign entered the closing days, Dewey appeared increasingly impatient to assume the prerogatives of the office. His attitude prompted one newsman to ask facetiously: "How long is Dewey going to tolerate Truman's interference in the government?" In his last campaign speech, in New York's Madison Square Garden, the Republican candidate radiated confidence and harmony: "I am very happy that we can look back over the weeks of our campaign and say: 'This has been good for our country.' I am proud that we can look ahead to our victory and say, 'America won.' " Truman kept slashing until the end. In one of his last speeches, he said he had been puzzled at first by Dewey's refusal to discuss the issues. "But after I had analyzed the situation," the President went on, "I came to the conclusion that the record of the Republican party is much too bad to talk about."

On the afternoon of Election Day, having made his closing speech from his home in Independence the night before, Truman slipped away to Excelsior Springs, Missouri, a resort town thirty-two miles away. He took a Turkish bath and went upstairs to his room. There the President of the United States dined alone on a ham sandwich and a glass of buttermilk, listened to some of the early returns, turned off his radio, and went to sleep.

The results that Truman had heard showed him in the lead. This was not surprising, because they came from traditional Democratic strongholds in the big cities of the East. But, as Republicans happily noted, Truman's margins were far from impressive. He carried Philadelphia, the first big city to report, by 6,000 votes, compared with Franklin Roosevelt's 150,000-vote majority there in 1944. Thus, at about 10:30 P.M. in Washington, while Truman slept in Excelsior Springs, Republican Chairman Scott confidently announced to the press: "Now we have come to the Republican half of the evening."

The trend Scott was waiting for, however, was notably slow to develop. While running neck and neck with Dewey in the East, Truman was showing surprising strength in the Republican bastions in the Midwest. One farm state after another—even, of all places, Iowa—was reporting Truman pluralities. It was past midnight in Excelsior Springs when the President awakened and tuned in commentator H. V. Kaltenborn. "I was about 1.2 million ahead on the count," the President remembered, "but according to this broadcaster, was still undoubtedly beaten." He switched off Kaltenborn and went back to sleep.

Meanwhile, Republican anxiety was growing, while the Democrats were finding more reason for hope. Truman had lost the three eastern kingpins, New York, New Jersey, and Pennsylvania. But in the hinterland beyond the Alleghenies, in the farm belt, the mountain states, and along the Pacific coast, he was more than making up for it. The South, most of it anyway, was proving itself loyal to the Democratic party.

In Excelsior Springs it was 4 A.M. when the President awoke again. On the radio, Kaltenborn continued to hold out against the Democratic tide. But the President was ahead by more than two million votes. He needed only Ohio or California to assure his triumph, and he was leading in both. That was enough for him. "We had better go back to Kansas City," he told his Secret Service guards; as he later wrote, "it looked very much as if we were in for another four years."

The issue remained in doubt until 10:30 A.M. eastern time, Wednesday, November 3, when Dewey formally conceded.

Truman received 303 electoral votes and 24.1 million popular votes to Dewey's 189 and 21.9 million. Thurmond and Wallace each got slightly more than 1.1 million votes, and Thurmond took 39 electoral votes —all from the South. With only 49.3 per cent of the popular vote, Truman was the first President since Woodrow Wilson in 1916 to be elected with less than a majority.

The most extraordinary thing about the election— other than the final outcome, of course—was the small turnout. Hundreds of thousands of Americans, evidently persuaded that their votes would make little difference in the net result, stayed away from the polls. The total presidential vote in 1948—48,687,607—was more than one million below the vote in the 1940 presidential election, although the population had grown by nearly 15 million (to 146 million) during the intervening eight years. And the 1948 vote was less than one million above the totals in the 1944 presidential election, although in 1944 the total population was smaller by 8 million, and 5.5 million Americans were overseas in the armed forces.

Neither the narrowness of his victory nor the low turnout of voters could diminish Truman's achievement. He had held Dewey to a lower percentage of the popular vote (44.9) than the Governor had gotten running against Roosevelt in 1944 (46.03). Moreover, the party Truman led had recaptured firm control of both houses of Congress and had wrested a net total of five governorships away from the Republicans.

The voters who had participated in this miracle could hardly believe the count of their own ballots. "If incredulity was ever written across the face of the nation," said Newsweek, "the election returns on Tuesday Nov. 2 certainly inscribed it indelibly there." Many faces were not only incredulous but red with embarrassment. A quick glance at the newsstands revealed how wrong everyone had been. The Chicago Tribune won an unsought—but probably richly deserved—niche in the annals of journalism with its banner headline: "Dewey Defeats Truman." In their

Mr. Shogan, who is a member of the staff of Newsweek, is the co-author of The Detroit Race Riot (Chilton, 1964).

For further reading: Out of the Jaws of Victory, by Jules Abels (Holt, 1959); The Truman Presidency, by Cabell Phillips (Macmillan, 1966); Memoirs, by Harry S. Truman (two volumes, Doubleday, 1955-56).

nationally syndicated column that appeared the day after the election, the Alsop brothers had solemnly written: "Events will not wait patiently until Thomas E. Dewey officially replaces Harry S. Truman." No major publication escaped the debacle, and one by one they apologized. On its front page, the Washington *Post* invited the President to a banquet attended by "political reporters and editors, including our own, along with pollsters, radio commentators and columnists.... The main course will consist of breast of tough old crow en glace. (You will eat turkey.)"

As for Dewey, he reacted with a grace and humor that would have benefited him during the campaign. On the day after the election, he told the press: "I am as much surprised as you are. I have read your stories. We were all wrong together." Later, Dewey was to say wryly that he felt like the man who woke up in a coffin with a lily in his hand and wondered: "If I am alive, what am I doing here? And if I'm dead, why do I have to go to the bathroom?"

Meanwhile, the rest of the nation was pondering a riddle just as perplexing. How had Truman managed to win? Or, as Republicans put it, how had Dewey managed to lose?

There are a number of possible answers. Truman's impassioned appeals to the labor and farm vote certainly played a major part in his victory. So did the natural appeal of the underdog and Truman's emergence during the campaign as a vigorous personality in his own right. The Wallace and Thurmond candidacies probably helped the President nearly as much as they hurt him, the former by drawing the fire of zealous anti-Communists and the latter by lending credibility to Truman's civil-rights programs.

Perhaps the most important single factor in Truman's victory was simply that he was President. Because he was President, he was able to make a nationwide "nonpolitical" campaign trip free of charge, to summon Congress into special session, and, in general, to command the attention and loyalty of the nation.

But what about Dewey? With the aid of hindsight, the commentators quickly pointed out where the Republican candidate had gone wrong. Had Dewey waged a more aggressive campaign, it was contended, the result would have been different. Indeed, it might have. But Dewey had based his strategy on the commonly accepted assumption that his victory was inevitable—a decision which, under the circumstances, had ample precedent in American politics. The underlying basis for this assumption was, of course, the unanimous verdict of the opinion polls.

The pollsters suffered more from the election results than anyone else, perhaps even more than the Republican party. But their humiliation offers prob-

ably the most enduring and encouraging lesson to be learned from the great upset of 1948: the folly of taking the American electorate for granted.

To find out why the pollsters had been so far off in their calculations, the Social Science Research Council appointed a committee of prominent educators to conduct a five-week investigation. Boiled down, the panel's 396-page verdict faulted the pollsters for neglecting to analyze the eventual decisions of undecided voters carefully enough, and for virtually ignoring shifts in sentiment at the end of the campaign. Finally, in presenting their results to the public, "the pollsters went far beyond the bounds of sound reporting.... They attempted the spectacular feat of predicting the winner without qualifications." In other words, as Elmo Roper said, he and his colleagues had been "honest, but dumb." Such predictions, the committee also charged, were not justified by the pollsters' past records. To be sure, they had all correctly picked Franklin Roosevelt to win the preceding three elections. But the average of their findings had consistently underestimated the Democratic vote. They had been spared embarrassment in the past only because Roosevelt had always won by a substantial margin.

A few days before the 1948 election, Democratic Chairman McGrath had reminded pollsters Crossley and Gallup of their past miscalculations and asked that they adjust their 1948 findings accordingly. Crossley said he found McGrath's objections "interesting" and expressed the hope that "we can sometime discuss these matters fully." Gallup was not nearly so polite. In just three words he unwittingly laid down a maxim that anyone trying to forecast an American election might well keep in mind.

What Gallup said was: "Wait till Tuesday!"

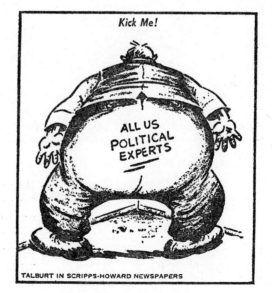

TALBURT IN SCRIPPS-HOWARD NEWSPAPERS

ZIP CODE
—1847

By DUDLEY C. GORDON

Some people—they tend to look upon mere stamp collectors with disdain—collect interesting envelopes; for example, those sent to or from persons of consequence. To such a collector the envelope reproduced below would probably bring a high fever of excitement. It was sent in June, 1847, from a famous United States senator who was a giant in the annals of the opening of the West, to his equally famous explorer-soldier son-in-law—and sent in care of a third man whose name has become as legendary as Davy Crockett's. Thomas Hart Benton, Missouri's first senator and still considered one of her greatest, was a big man physically, mentally, and politically. He never flagged in his determination to see the American nation reach out to embrace Oregon, California, and the vast Southwest. When his daughter Jessie eloped in 1841 with a handsome and dynamic young army lieutenant named John Charles Frémont, Senator Benton was soon reconciled by the ardor with which Frémont conducted several important exploring expeditions westward. One of them ended, in 1846, with action against the Mexicans at Sonoma and the first raising of California's Bear Flag as the ensign of independence from Mexico. Christopher "Kit" Carson was Frémont's chief guide on that expedition and on others; as a result of Frémont's enthusiastic reports, his name too became an exciting one for stay-at-home Americans. By June of 1847, Frémont was in trouble, having quarrelled with tough old Stephen Watts Kearny, the conqueror of California—in fact, he was on his way east to face a court-martial for insubordination. (Frémont was convicted—unjustly, many thought; he remained famous and popular.) Senator Benton, tremendously vague as to his son-in-law's exact whereabouts, addressed a letter on June 22, 1847, from Fort Leavenworth (then in Missouri) to "Lt. Col. Frémont, New Mexico, or California" assuring him that his family was well and eagerly awaiting his return. As an afterthought and in view of the uncertainties of mail service on the wild frontier, the Senator added: "Care of Mr. C. Carson." It was a very primitive zip code, but apparently effective: the letter eventually reached the addressee. It now reposes in the Southwest Museum in Los Angeles.